FUTURE NARRATOR

TRANSFORM YOUR THOUGHT LEADERSHIP INTO A GLOBAL MOVEMENT

EDWIN J.FRONDOZO   DR. PAUL NEWTON

FUTURE NARRATOR

ISBN-13: 978-1-990476-15-0

Published by: Expert Author Press

https://www.expertauthorpress.com/

Canadian Address:

767 Eastvale Dr

Ottawa, ON K1J 6Z9

Phone: (604) 941-3041

info@expertauthorpress.com

Dedication

For my parents, whose unconditional love and tireless support have shaped the path to my future.

Edwin

To my parents, whose unwavering love and support laid the foundation for a future that continues to flourish with every step I take.

Paul

TABLE OF CONTENTS

PART 1

INTRODUCTION

What if a single bold declaration could transform your leadership, redefine your company, and inspire a movement that changes the way the world sees your industry? This book introduces the Future Narrator framework, a transformative process that empowers founder CEOs to refine their thought leadership, align their vision and values, and inspire meaningful change. By following a clear, step-by-step method rooted in focused execution and iterative refinement, you will discover how to turn effortless conversations into strategic outcomes, build legacy assets like books and podcasts, and foster a profound connection with your community and industry. The journey begins with a bold declaration, and the outcomes are nothing short of revolutionary.

Matt Bertulli, the founder of Lomi, made the bold statement, "What if you could get rid of your trash at the push of a button?" He reimagined waste management as something effortless, rewarding, and accessible to anyone—even those living in small apartments. By positioning Lomi as a simple push-button solution, he turned composting from a messy, inconvenient chore into an empowering act of environmental responsibility. More than just a product, he framed a future where sustainability was easy, inspiring an entire community to adopt his vision. His ability to compellingly tell this story and rally people behind it is precisely what sets Future Narrators apart. They don't just compete in existing categories. They create and mobilize new ones. We'll talk more about Matt in the next chapter.

The Future Narrator Framework came to life when Paul and I first met in late 2021. It was clear that our skill sets complemented each other in a way that could create something powerful. I had a bold vision and a structured execution approach, while Paul had the ability to systematize ideas, refine narratives, and turn complex concepts into digestible content. Our connection started when he attended my webinar on planning the first 100 days of 2022, where I shared how a bold declaration to 100X my telecom business in 100 days had transformed my life. Paul immediately saw the potential in the structured framework behind my goal and recognized a disciplined way to channel multi-passionate energy into extraordinary results. As we continued our conversations, we realized that combining my expertise in podcasting and thought leadership with his structured content development and publishing experience could help leaders carve out their own category and mobilize movements.

As we explored the idea further, we saw a clear opportunity to help founder CEOs become Future Narrators—leaders who don't just compete in existing categories but create and mobilize new ones. Paul had already successfully turned a series of employment branding webinars into a book that helped position himself and his business partner as an authority in their industry. Inspired by this, I wondered if The Business Leadership Podcast, which I launched as a business growth strategy for my telecom company Slingshot in 2017, could be used for something similar. With over 200 episodes and conversations, Paul assured me it could become a cohesive narrative that would serve as both thought leadership and a lasting legacy. That realization led us to develop a structured process to guide leaders through articulating their unique Point of View (POV), establishing their thought leadership, and leveraging their insights to build communities and movements around their ideas. Refining this process, we discovered that defining a category involved activating it through strategic content, storytelling, and engagement.

Our research into category creation deepened, with Paul studying works like "The Category Pirates" by Christopher Lochhead and his co-authors. At the same time, I immersed myself in industry insights from leading voices in the space. To refine our understanding, we invited key experts to my Business Leadership Podcast, including

Mike Damphousse, whose perspectives on category creation were transformative. Through these discussions, we identified our niche: category mobilization. Unlike traditional category creation, which focuses on defining a space, category mobilization ensures that a category is activated and sustained through ongoing engagement, community-building, and the creation of legacy assets. This became the foundation of the Future Narrator framework—a methodical approach for founder CEOs to use thought leadership to inspire change, establish industry influence, and create movements that redefine markets.

Purpose of the Book

This book is our guide to showing founder CEOs how to become Future Narrators—leaders who redefine their industries by owning a category through thought leadership, mobilization, and evangelization. Following the Future Narrator Framework developed through our combined expertise, you'll refine your vision, craft a clear Point of View (POV), and align your leadership, business, and community to create meaningful change and inspire movements.

Diagram Overview

This diagram provides a high-level view of the **Future Narrator Framework**, showing how a clear future vision, active community engagement, and enduring content (the three overlapping circles) come together to create thought leadership with lasting impact. The center represents the core idea—shaping a future-focused narrative—while the outer sections illustrate how this narrative, once developed, can achieve momentum, longevity, and influence. The framework depicted here will serve as the foundation for exploring how to become a Future Narrator throughout the rest of this book.

Strategic Visioning

Developing and refining a unique Future POV that sets the foundation for thought leadership.

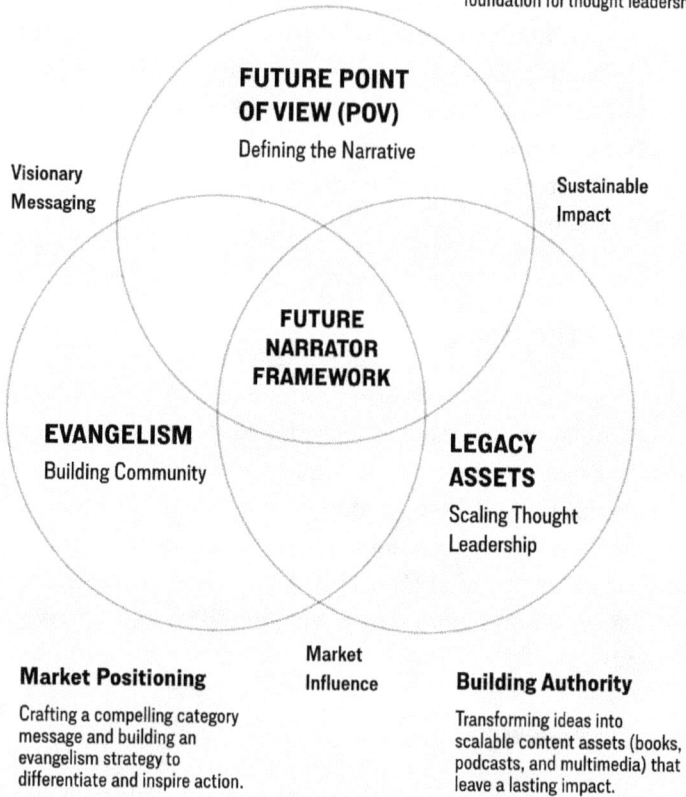

FUTURE POINT OF VIEW (POV)

Defining the Narrative

Visionary Messaging

Sustainable Impact

FUTURE NARRATOR FRAMEWORK

EVANGELISM

Building Community

LEGACY ASSETS

Scaling Thought Leadership

Market Influence

Market Positioning

Crafting a compelling category message and building an evangelism strategy to differentiate and inspire action.

Building Authority

Transforming ideas into scalable content assets (books, podcasts, and multimedia) that leave a lasting impact.

Figure 1. Future Narrator Framework

How the Book is Structured

This book is divided into two parts. The first part, Chapters 1 to 6, walks you through the Future Narrator Framework, giving you a step-by-step process to transform into a thought leader who mobilizes your category.

In Chapter 1, you will start by understanding the importance of a strong Point of View (POV) and how it serves as the foundation for industry leadership. Chapter 2 will guide you in crafting your Future Narrative, a compelling story that aligns your vision, values, and purpose to inspire change. In Chapter 3, you will learn how to evangelize your category, transforming your vision into a movement that gains traction and impact. Chapter 4 explores the power of podcasting as a tool for thought leadership, allowing you to expand your reach and refine your message. Chapter 5 will show you how to turn that content into a book, creating a lasting legacy that cements your authority in your industry. Finally, Chapter 6 combines everything into a structured, repeatable process that allows you to continually evolve, engage your audience, and create lasting influence.

The second part highlights the profiles of 20 incredible thought leaders we interviewed live on our podcast at Collision Conference 2024 in Toronto. How we produced these profiles demonstrates how the framework works in real-world scenarios and provides proof of concept for the ideas in this book.

How to Use This Book

Each chapter of this book provides critical steps in the Future Narrator Framework, ending with key takeaways and actionable steps. To help you work through each phase, we've included downloadable worksheets that you can use to apply what you've learned.

There are two ways you can approach this book:

1. Chapter by chapter, working through the process step by step, completing the worksheets as you go.

2. Read the book for an overview, absorbing the entire framework, and then return to the worksheets later.

We've also created a comprehensive process worksheet for each chapter and a complete workbook available for download. This resource provides a full start-to-finish view of the system. Whether you prefer a detailed, methodical approach or a high-level overview, this book is designed to meet your needs while providing a complete roadmap for success.

By the end of this book, you will understand the Future Narrator Framework and be equipped to implement it, positioning yourself as a leader with the power to shape the future.

We're inviting you to take this journey to become a Future Narrator—to refine your thought leadership, inspire a movement, and create lasting change. This is your chance to share your bold vision with the world, own your category, and build a platform that aligns with your values and aspirations. With the tools and frameworks in this book, you'll have everything you need to start your journey and leave an enduring legacy. Let's get started.

CHAPTER 1

Thought Leadership—The Road to Category Creation

Thought Leadership Starts with a Point of View (POV)

In today's competitive and fast-paced landscape, having the most innovative product or solution is no longer enough to stand out. Success depends on the ability to answer a more fundamental question: Why does this matter to me? Startups with brilliant ideas often fail because they cannot connect their innovations to the needs, values, or aspirations of their audience or investors. In contrast, leaders like Marc Benioff of Salesforce illustrate the transformative power of a bold Point of View (POV). Benioff didn't just introduce a leading customer relationship management (CRM) platform—he redefined the software industry by pioneering cloud computing.

Benioff's POV—that business could be a platform for social change—challenged entrenched industry norms. Before Salesforce, businesses accepted complex, costly, and time-consuming on-premise software installations as inevitable. Benioff envisioned a different future where software was accessible, scalable, and aligned with meaningful outcomes like customer success and social impact. His promotion of software as a service (SaaS) exposed inefficiencies in traditional models and delighted customers with solutions they hadn't even realized they needed. This wasn't just about delivering better software; it was about reshaping what companies could achieve with technology and inspiring a global movement that went beyond CRM.

Why Founders and CEOs Must Lead with POV

In an oversaturated market, the leaders who rise above are those who articulate a clear and authentic POV. A strong POV reflects a deep understanding of market needs while challenging conventional thinking. It positions leaders as Future Narrators—visionaries who can see beyond present challenges and chart a bold path forward. These are the leaders who redefine their industries rather than merely compete within them.

This chapter explores how a well-articulated POV can become the foundation for transformative leadership. By adopting and communicating a bold perspective, leaders have the power to attract loyal followers, influence industry narratives, and drive meaningful change. Are you ready to lead with your own compelling POV, create your category, and leave a lasting impact on the world?

POV as a Bold Statement

A Point of View (POV) is more than just a belief; it's a statement of what truly matters to a leader. It's the driving force behind bold leadership, enabling individuals to challenge norms and redefine the future. A compelling POV requires courage—standing firm on perspectives that may be provocative or even unpopular but are grounded in authenticity. This boldness compels others to question their assumptions and aligns them with a greater vision.

Thought leadership requires a willingness to challenge the status quo. Leaders with a bold POV don't settle for incremental changes; they aim to overhaul broken systems. During my conversation with Michael Katchen on The Business Leadership Podcast, his passion for breaking down barriers to investing was unmistakable. For Michael, Wealthsimple wasn't just about simplifying the investment process but fundamentally changing how the financial industry operated. His belief that investing should be simple and accessible to everyone—not just the wealthy or financially savvy—challenged deeply ingrained practices and highlighted the exclusivity of traditional financial models. His vision sparked a movement, transforming wealth-building into an opportunity for all.

There's a significant difference between enhancing what already exists and truly challenging it. Enhancements may bring incremental improvements, but transformative leadership breaks entirely new ground. This approach is often risky, uncomfortable, and met with resistance—but it's where real change happens. Leaders who dare to challenge must ask themselves, "What do I believe about this industry that no one else does?" Answering this question and standing by it with conviction separates true innovators from followers.

Turning POV into Thought Leadership

Having a compelling Point of View (POV) is one thing, but turning it into effective thought leadership is another. The key is relevance: making beliefs resonate with others. Founders must consider their audience—how does their POV intersect with the audience's challenges, aspirations, and realities? A strong POV makes others care. It's not enough to declare a belief; leaders must communicate why it matters to their audience's experiences. This means understanding the issues that resonate most with stakeholders—customers, employees, partners, and the broader community—and linking the leader's perspective to shared challenges.

In my podcast interview with Matthew Bertulli, co-founder of Pela Case and Lomi, his passion for sustainability and innovation offered a clear example of connecting a POV to the audience. Matthew explained that, beyond creating eco-friendly products, his vision was about empowering people to take small, meaningful steps toward reducing global waste. By aligning his company's mission with the growing concern for environmental responsibility, he fostered a loyal community of customers who saw themselves as contributors to a sustainable future. His POV resonated because it wasn't just about products; it was about driving systemic change.

Thought Leadership as an Active Process

Thought leadership is an active, ongoing process requiring consistent engagement. Founders and CEOs must share their POV repeatedly across platforms—articles, podcasts, speeches, and public discussions that align with their vision. Each opportunity builds credibility and visibility and gradually establishes a distinct place in the market conversation. Consistency is crucial—a strong POV gains power through repeated exposure. The more consistently a founder shares their POV, the more likely they are to shape the market narrative.

During our discussion, Matthew described how sharing his vision for sustainability across diverse platforms became essential to building trust and momentum. Articles, keynote speeches, and collaborations with environmental influencers amplified Lomi's mission, transforming composting from a chore into an empowering act of global impact. By consistently sharing his beliefs and vision, Matthew positioned himself and Lomi as leaders in the sustainability movement, inspiring customers, partners, and even competitors to join the effort. By actively sharing their beliefs, founders position themselves as voices of influence, attracting followers—customers, partners, employees, and investors—ultimately leading to category ownership.

From POV to Movement

The ultimate goal of thought leadership is to create a movement—mobilizing others around an idea. Thought leaders drive action, encouraging others to see the world differently and act accordingly. To achieve this, founders must communicate their vision in a way that inspires others, showing how adopting this perspective can lead to meaningful change.

Matthew highlighted how Lomi's success was rooted in educating and inspiring customers to see waste management as part of a bigger story. Through storytelling and strategic partnerships, he reframed composting as an empowering act of environmental responsibility. By consistently sharing this vision across multiple platforms, he built a community of advocates who felt personally invested in the mission. Founders like Matthew, shape industry narratives to reflect their vision this way.

Building a Story Around POV

A powerful Point of View (POV) becomes transformative when framed within a compelling story. Storytelling brings the leader's vision to life, helping others understand the POV and why it matters. A story explains the "why" behind the perspective, transforming abstract beliefs into a vivid narrative that resonates on a human level.

People connect with stories because they evoke emotion and inspire empathy. When a founder shares how they arrived at their POV, it humanizes them, allowing audiences to see their motivations, struggles, and passion. This personal touch makes the POV accessible and relatable, shifting the narrative from a set of facts to an experience that invites others to see the world differently.

In my conversation with Matthew, I found his passion for sustainability and innovation inspiring. Beyond creating eco-friendly products, he spoke about empowering individuals to make small, meaningful choices that collectively lead to significant environmental change. Frustrated by the overwhelming amount of waste generated by consumer products, he began to reimagine everyday items to reduce global waste. Matthew created a relatable and emotionally resonant narrative that inspired both customers and partners to care about the growing concerns around sustainability.

Stories evoke reflection and encourage critical thinking They invite audiences to ask, "Why have we been doing things this way for so long?" Emotional engagement is essential for effective thought leadership. Audiences must not only understand the leader's perspective but also feel it and internalize it as meaningful.

Matthew's story of developing Lomi to solve waste management inefficiencies struck a chord with environmentally conscious consumers. He reframed composting from an inconvenient chore to an empowering action anyone could take to reduce their carbon footprint. This emotional hook made the vision memorable, turning customers into advocates for sustainability.

Crafting a Compelling Narrative

A strong narrative around a POV should include:

1. **The Origin:** Share where the POV came from—what personal experience, observation, or challenge led to this belief.

    *   Example: Matthew's realization of the unsustainable nature of consumer products and his determination to create alternatives like Pela Case and Lomi.

2. **The Challenge:** Identify what's wrong with the status quo. Why is the current way insufficient? Use examples to illustrate why change is necessary.

    *   Example: Traditional composting was inaccessible and inefficient, deterring people from adopting eco-friendly habits.

3. **The Vision:** Show the future that could be, thanks to your POV. Help the audience visualize the impact and how their world might improve.

    *   Example: A future where everyday choices, like using compostable products, significantly reduce global waste.

4. **Emotional Hooks:** Use anecdotes that make the audience feel. These elements make the vision personal and memorable.

    *   Example: Sharing customer stories about how Lomi transformed their perspective on sustainability.

The goal of storytelling in thought leadership is to inspire action. When audiences see themselves in the story, they are more likely to take the next step—to join the movement, share the vision, or change their behaviours. The leader's role is to help others imagine a new possibility and feel excited about being part of that change.

Matthew Bertulli's example shows how a founder can inspire collective action. By creating a community around his products and educating people about sustainability, he transformed customers into collaborators in his mission to reduce waste.

Passion and the Power of Contrarian Views

Passion drives every impactful Point of View (POV). For a POV to stand out and position a founder or CEO as a thought leader, it often needs to be contrarian—going against mainstream thinking. True thought leadership challenges norms, questions the status quo, and proposes a new way forward. This willingness to think boldly and differently separates category creators from industry participants.

Thought leaders are change agents. They voice perspectives that contradict accepted norms, speaking out when others hesitate. They advocate ideas others may find radical, uncomfortable, or even threatening. This boldness attracts attention, resonates with those seeking change, and builds a following for a new future.

During my conversation with Michael Katchen, he challenged the deeply entrenched belief that financial services must remain complex and exclusive, arguing that simplicity and accessibility are key. Michael has made the traditional barriers of wealth-building glaringly obvious, promoting the idea that anyone can invest and benefit from financial growth. His vision redefined who participates, inspiring a broader movement toward financial inclusivity.

A contrarian POV is risky—it goes against collective wisdom and often faces strong resistance. True thought leaders recognize that to change an industry or create a new market, they must endure the discomfort of standing apart. Passion fuels these leaders, allowing them to persist through obstacles, ultimately leading to breakthroughs.

Michael relentlessly focused on demystifying investing through Wealthsimple. His decision to focus on younger, less experienced investors rather than the wealthy elite traditionally served by financial institutions was not only contrarian but transformative. This passion for inclusivity and innovation allowed him to build a loyal community of first-time investors.

Leaders must be encouraged to voice their contrarian perspectives with conviction. The world doesn't need more of the same; it needs innovative thinkers who stand for something different. Thought leadership is about envisioning a radically different future and having the courage to lead others there. Leaders can carve out a unique market position by being vocal about bold, controversial beliefs.

Michael's passion for breaking down the barriers to financial growth resonates across every Wealthsimple initiative. From socially responsible investment options to intuitive user interfaces, his commitment to empowering everyday people with tools previously reserved for the elite is evident. This passion inspires trust and motivates others to embrace his vision of financial democratization.

Passion must be palpable in a thought leader's words, actions, and consistent communication across platforms. A passionate, contrarian POV draws people in and inspires them to support and participate in building a movement.

Envisioning a New World Through POV

An impactful Point of View (POV) paints a vivid picture of the future. Thought leaders help others envision a world where their perspective becomes reality. This new world represents the solution to an industry-wide problem or the fulfillment of an untapped opportunity, providing clarity and hope while inviting others to share in the vision.

For a POV to create a movement, it must show what is possible—helping people see beyond current limitations and imagine a transformed industry, lifestyle, or society. This future should feel attainable yet transformative, motivating others to embrace the leader's vision. For example, Matthew Bertulli shares a vision of a future where waste is no longer a burden but a resource that fuels sustainability. His narrative isn't just about composting with Lomi—it's about changing how households and businesses think about waste management and their environmental impact. By painting this bold picture, Bertulli inspires consumers to see themselves as active participants in reducing global waste and supporting a circular economy.

Make it Vivid: Illustrate the Benefits

To engage people with your POV, make the vision tangible. Use storytelling to show how this new world benefits your audience and solves problems they may not realize they have. Move beyond abstract ideas and offer concrete examples—how it feels, functions, and why it is better than the present. Matthew Bertulli reimagined how people interact with waste, painting a future where composting is a simple, seamless part of everyday life. With Lomi, people can turn organic waste into usable soil overnight with the push of a button, even in an apartment, making sustainability both effortless and impactful. By making this vision vivid, he turned waste management from an afterthought into an accessible, inspiring action that people want to participate in.

A powerful POV should carve out a new category. It must be bold enough to address a gap that the market hasn't recognized, highlighting a problem most have accepted or overlooked and proposing a different solution that needs new space to thrive. Category creation is driven by understanding latent needs and emerging opportunities. Founders who recognize these gaps can use their POV to define a new category, reframing market norms. By consistently articulating this bold perspective, they reframe the market conversation and highlight opportunities others missed.

Once a new category is established, it's essential to tie it back to the company's core mission. The POV should reflect the organization's purpose, ensuring authenticity and a strong foundation aligned with the company's values and goals. The core mission acts as a guiding force, keeping the company focused on leading the category consistently.

Connecting Storytelling to Your Future Narrative

This chapter has explored how a clear and compelling Point of View (POV) becomes the foundation for thought leadership, category creation, and movement-building. By framing your POV within a powerful story, you transform it into something that resonates deeply with customers, employees, partners, and stakeholders. A strong POV, communicated through storytelling, has the power to inspire action and redefine entire industries. Pela, Lomi's parent company, had reported selling over 200,000 units as of mid 2023, creating the new category of in-home, electric composting, which was previously an underserved segment of the market.

Marc Benioff's journey with Salesforce illustrates how a bold POV and a well-crafted narrative can solve hidden problems, challenge the status quo, and build an engaged community by redefining software delivery through cloud computing. Michael Katchen's commitment to financial accessibility with Wealthsimple highlights how a contrarian view can dismantle traditional barriers and invite a broader audience into wealth-building opportunities. Meanwhile, Matthew Bertulli's dedication to sustainability through Lomi demonstrates how a leader's vision can transform everyday practices, like composting, into impactful actions that address global environmental challenges. Each leader shows how a clear POV, communicated effectively, can disrupt industries, solve meaningful problems, and create lasting movements that inspire change.

A strong POV must solve unspoken challenges, align with your audience's aspirations, and invite them to become part of the solution. It's not enough to present a product or service—you must position it within a larger narrative that inspires connection and action. As your company grows, your story must evolve, always staying true to the core vision and values that define your POV.

With your POV firmly established and framed within a story that drives connection, the next step is to expand this into a Future Narrative. This narrative will go beyond defining your current mission and instead paint a vivid picture of where you are heading, the movement you are building, and how others can join you. In Chapter 2, we'll explore how to craft a Future Narrative that mobilizes employees, customers, and partners to actively participate in shaping the future you envision. Let's take the next step in turning your POV into a vision that redefines your industry and inspires the world.

Defining Your Thought Leadership & POV
Download the Chapter Worksheet

Refine your thought leadership and define your unique POV
with this worksheet.

resources.futurenarrator.com/pov

CHAPTER 2

Creating Your Future Narrative

The Power of a Future Narrative

Yvon Chouinard imagined a world where businesses didn't just extract from the planet but actively worked to protect it. He envisioned companies as stewards of the environment, leading the charge against climate change and inspiring others to do the same. Guided by this vision, Chouinard transformed Patagonia into a symbol of environmental responsibility and corporate activism. From donating 1% of sales to environmental causes to transferring ownership of Patagonia to a trust dedicated to preserving the planet, his actions embodied his story of what the world could be. This is what we call a Future Narrative—a compelling vision that not only defines a company's direction but also inspires movements that create lasting change. What could your Future Narrative achieve?

In Chapter 1, we explored the significance of defining your Point of View (POV)—the unique perspective that serves as the foundation of your leadership and thought leadership strategy. Your POV is the lens through which you interpret your role in your industry and the broader world. In Chapter 2, we take this foundational perspective and use it to craft your Future Narrative, a transformative story that defines where you're heading and inspires others to join you.

A Future Narrative represents the decision by founder CEOs to lead with a purpose that goes beyond products, inspiring a movement and inviting others to see the future differently. By crafting and living their Future Narrative, leaders will see a company culture driven by alignment and purpose, where daily operations reflect the shared vision, teams act with clarity and passion, and stakeholders engage as active participants in a transformative movement.

A Future Narrative aligns purpose, innovation, and action into a cohesive framework that inspires others to join in building a shared future. It is visionary and forward-looking, painting a vivid picture of what's possible and inspiring excitement about the change being created. Grounded in deeply held values, it ensures authenticity and resonance. A strong Future Narrative is also relatable and inclusive, inviting employees, customers, and partners to see themselves in the story. Finally, it is action-oriented, bridging the gap between aspiration and tangible steps to achieve the vision.

This chapter will guide you through crafting your Future Narrative by breaking it into clear and actionable steps. You will learn how to define your future vision to establish a compelling foundation, craft a strategic story that connects and inspires, and make your narrative personal and authentic to build trust and credibility. Additionally, you will explore how to create a shared future that invites collaboration and participation and how to bring your narrative to life through meaningful actions aligned with your vision.

By the end of this chapter, you'll discover what's possible when you create a Future Narrative. This transformative story defines your company's direction and propels you to inspire others, and lead with purpose. Imagine the impact of a compelling future vision that aligns your team, engages your stakeholders, and sets you apart as a catalyst of global transformation.

Defining the Future Vision

Your POV provides the lens through which you imagine what's possible, and your future vision translates that perspective into a clear, actionable narrative. This vision bridges the gap between who you are and the transformative change you want to lead, serving as the cornerstone of your Future Narrative.

To create a Future Narrative that truly resonates, you must first define your future vision—a vision that guides your company and reimagines your industry's landscape. This future vision is the cornerstone of the narrative you want to build; it goes beyond short-term goals or internal mission statements, reaching toward a broader purpose that inspires both your organization and the world around you. A compelling future vision is aspirational and transformative—it paints a picture of how things could be different and how the world could improve and invites others to help make that vision a reality.

I first met Victoria Lennox after I launched Slingshot. It was clear that I needed to network and connect with communities that shared my entrepreneurial spirit to grow. At the time, Startup Canada was launching, and they put out a call for volunteers. I joined and managed two of their key programs—100 Startups, which profiled emerging businesses, and #StartupChats, a popular Twitter chat that brought entrepreneurs together online. Working closely with Victoria, I became a trusted team member, and our relationship grew.

So, when I launched The Business Leadership Podcast, still seeking a deeper connection with entrepreneurs, Victoria was one of the first people I reached out to. On March 28, 2017, she appeared in Episode 2 of the show, sharing her incredible vision for Canada's entrepreneurial future. It was about transforming Canada into an innovation nation. She imagined a future where starting and scaling a business was accessible to everyone, regardless of geography or background. Her vision extended far beyond the traditional focus on urban startup hubs, emphasizing inclusivity and collaboration nationwide. She inspired grassroots entrepreneurial communities, forged partnerships with government and private organizations, and redefined what it means to build a thriving entrepreneurial ecosystem. Her Future Narrative invites others—entrepreneurs, policymakers, and citizens—to envision and contribute to a future where innovation drives economic growth and strengthens communities.

To articulate your future vision, start by asking yourself: What transformation do you want to see in your industry? How will your company contribute to the changes that must take place? Your future vision should be ambitious yet tangible, providing a clear direction that everyone—from employees to customers—can rally behind. It is about understanding today's problems and imagining a better future that your company is uniquely positioned to create.

Reflection exercises can help here. Write down the aspects of your industry that feel stagnant or outdated. Imagine what the future looks like if those problems are solved—what does that new world look like? What role will your company play in bringing that vision to life? The answers to these questions will help you shape a future vision that is not only clear but also deeply meaningful, both to you and to those you wish to inspire.

A future vision must be bold enough to challenge the status quo, breaking away from "business as usual" to spark excitement and invite others to follow. By embracing a transformative future vision, you position yourself as a leader, unafraid to imagine a better way forward and inspire others to make it happen.

Crafting the Strategic Story

Jeff Ruby is one of the most fascinating entrepreneurs I've had the chance to meet. His future vision for healthcare—a proactive system designed to prevent chronic diseases—resonated deeply with what I want for myself and my family and inspired me to reach out to him and invite him on my show. His company, Newtopia, has turned this vision into a reality, proving that healthcare can focus on empowerment and prevention rather than reaction.

Once you have defined your future vision, the next step is to craft a strategic story that brings that vision to life. To illustrate this process, we'll explore each component of the strategic story structure through the lens of Jeff Ruby's Future Narrative. By examining the disruption, his contrast between the present world and future world, the roles of anchors and evolvers, and the tools and signals that propel his vision forward, we can see how a well-crafted narrative turns a vision into a movement that inspires belief and action.

The Disruption

The disruption is the undeniable shift that makes it impossible for people to continue operating the same way and expecting the same results. For Jeff Ruby, this disruption is the alarming rise in lifestyle-related diseases and the skyrocketing costs of treating preventable conditions. More people than ever are suffering from chronic illnesses such as diabetes and heart disease, eroding their quality of life despite advancements in medicine, increased affluence, and more leisure time. This crisis has created an unsustainable burden on individuals, families, and the healthcare system. Jeff's Future Narrative exposes this reality and presents a bold new path—shifting from reactive treatment to proactive prevention, where individuals are empowered with personalized tools to take control of their health before illness takes hold. This disruption is the foundation of Jeff's strategic story—it makes the case for why change is necessary and why the old way can no longer sustain a thriving society.

Present World vs. Future World

The present world represents the reality that people are struggling to navigate, clinging to outdated strategies that no longer serve them. Even as disruption unfolds, many continue attempting to solve problems with the same approaches, leaving them frustrated and unfulfilled. They are caught in a cycle of escalating challenges, desperately trying to maintain control while their environment shifts beneath them. The future world, on the other hand, presents a new way of being—one where the disruption has been addressed, and individuals can move forward with clarity and confidence. This future world is not just an abstract possibility; it is made tangible through a compelling Future Narrative that bridges the gap between uncertainty and transformation.

In the present world, healthcare is focused on treating symptoms, with skyrocketing costs and limited emphasis on prevention. This results in an unsustainable system that reacts to illness rather than working to prevent it in the first place. Jeff Ruby's Future Narrative envisions a future world where chronic diseases are rare, and individuals are equipped with personalized tools to lead healthier lives. His story illustrates how proactive healthcare can empower individuals to take control of their well-being, improving quality of life and reducing costs for businesses and society as a whole. By contrasting these two worlds, Jeff makes it glaringly obvious that staying in the present world will only lead to worsening health outcomes and financial strain, while embracing the future world opens the door to a sustainable, thriving healthcare model.

Anchors and Evolvers

Every transformative story has its anchors—those who resist change—and its evolvers—those who embrace the vision and lead the way. The key is to show the real cost of resisting change so that people naturally choose to evolve rather than feeling blamed for their struggles. In Jeff's narrative, anchors are those clinging to an outdated healthcare model that prioritizes expensive treatments over prevention. They continue down an unsustainable path, facing skyrocketing healthcare costs, worsening health outcomes, and an increasing inability to enjoy the quality of life they've worked so hard to achieve.

Meanwhile, evolvers—employers, insurers, and individuals who recognize the shift—are thriving by embracing preventative care and investing in solutions like Newtopia's programs. The choice is clear: staying anchored to the old way will only lead to financial and physical decline, while those who evolve will navigate the disruption and move toward a healthier, more sustainable future. By positioning Newtopia as a partner for evolvers, Jeff makes it clear that the path forward is not about resisting change but about thriving in a transformed world.

The World Transformed

The world transformed is the promised land—the undeniable proof that the disruption has paved the way for a new and better reality. It is not just an improvement; it is an entirely different way of living, one where the struggles of the present world are left behind, and individuals can thrive in ways they never imagined possible. This vision should be so enticing, so undeniably better, that people naturally want to step into it. They must see that staying in the present world will only lead to frustration, struggle, and decline, whereas embracing the future world will open doors to prosperity, health, and fulfillment. This is the power of a Future Narrative—it makes the choice clear and compelling, inspiring people to move forward with confidence.

For Jeff Ruby, this world transformed is a society where chronic diseases like diabetes and heart disease are dramatically reduced, healthcare costs are lowered, and individuals lead healthier, more fulfilling lives. Instead of spending their later years battling preventable conditions, people can enjoy the fruits of their labor, fully experiencing their wealth, time, and relationships without being limited by poor health. His Future Narrative paints this picture so vividly that the choice becomes obvious—those who evolve will thrive in this new reality, while those who resist change will continue struggling with rising healthcare costs, declining health, and a lower quality of life.

Catalyst Tools

Catalyst tools are how you position your features and benefits as powerful enablers of transformation. These tools are not just products or services; they are the essential mechanisms that allow people to transition from the present world of struggle and frustration into the future world where they thrive. Without them, navigating the disruption would feel impossible, but with them, people are empowered to embrace the change and step into a better way of living.

In Jeff Ruby's Future Narrative, Newtopia's catalyst tools make this transformation possible. His personalized health programs integrate genetic, social, and behavioral insights to help individuals prevent chronic diseases rather than merely treating them. These tools equip people with the knowledge, support, and structure they need to take control of their health, dramatically reducing the risks of diabetes, heart disease, and other lifestyle-related illnesses. For employers and insurers, these catalyst tools provide a scalable solution to improve employee health, lower healthcare costs, and enhance productivity. By framing Newtopia's services as essential catalyst tools, Jeff positions his company as the key partner in helping people and organizations transition into the future world of preventative healthcare, where well-being and longevity replace avoidable suffering and expense.

Momentum Signals

Momentum signals represent the proof that your Future Narrative has gained traction. They show that your future vision is actively guiding people toward the world transformed, demonstrating that the promised future is not just aspirational—it is already happening. These signals provide the social proof that when people use your catalyst tools, they successfully escape the struggles of the disruption and reach the better reality you've envisioned. For Newtopia, these momentum signals include compelling success stories from individuals who have reclaimed their health through personalized prevention programs, measurable reductions in healthcare costs for businesses, and partnerships with Fortune 500 companies that have adopted this proactive model. These signals reinforce the inevitability of the future world and inspire confidence that joining the movement is the best choice for those who want to thrive.

By structuring your strategic story around these components, you create a narrative that is compelling and actionable. Jeff Ruby's example illustrates how a well-crafted strategic story can transform a future vision into a movement that resonates with audiences and drives meaningful change.

Making the Narrative Personal

A Future Narrative must be deeply personal to the leader sharing it to truly resonate. When founders make their narrative personal, it becomes authentic, relatable, and trustworthy. Audiences connect with leaders who show vulnerability, share their motivations, and speak from their experiences. By weaving personal elements into your Future Narrative, you provide a more profound emotional layer that makes your vision more inspiring and relatable.

Victoria's vision to transform Canada into an innovation nation was deeply rooted in her personal experiences, including the life-changing challenges she faced while battling cancer. When I first connected with Victoria, she shared how her diagnosis of Hodgkin's lymphoma during her time at Oxford taught her to lead from behind, empowering her team while stepping back from the spotlight. This formative experience shaped her leadership philosophy of collaboration, trust, and community-driven success. It also fueled her unwavering passion for creating opportunities for others, building an entrepreneurial ecosystem that is inclusive and supportive. By sharing her journey of resilience, from triumphs to setbacks, she made her Future Narrative deeply relatable and inspiring, forging authentic connections with entrepreneurs, policymakers, and communities across Canada.

To make your narrative personal, reflect on what truly drives you. Why does this future vision matter to you? Think back to key moments in your life—experiences that shaped your values, defined your perspective, or ignited your passion for change. These moments are the building blocks of an authentic narrative. By sharing them, you humanize your story and invite others to understand what you are striving for and why it matters so deeply.

Being personal also means being open about challenges. No journey is without its setbacks, and sharing yours makes your narrative more relatable. People admire leaders who are willing to be vulnerable and share not just their successes but also their struggles. This shows resilience, determination, and a genuine commitment to making a difference despite obstacles.

A personal narrative is about creating a connection. When people see the passion and sincerity behind your words, they feel more inclined to join you, trust you, and share in your vision. Make sure your narrative highlights the human aspect—yours and those of the people you are striving to impact—and you will find that your Future Narrative becomes far more compelling, inspiring those around you to believe and participate in your journey.

Creating a Shared Future

A Future Narrative has its most significant impact when it moves beyond the leader and becomes a shared vision that invites employees, customers, partners, and communities to participate. Creating a shared future means developing a narrative where others can see themselves—making them feel they are a necessary part of the journey. A Future Narrative should inspire and engage others in its realization, creating a sense of collective ownership in shaping that future.

Jeff Ruby envisioned Newtopia as a movement to revolutionize how chronic diseases are prevented. He invited employers, insurers, and individuals to join in reshaping the healthcare system, empowering them to become co-creators of a healthier society. Employers became partners in fostering preventative care and reducing healthcare costs. Insurers were engaged as advocates for a proactive health model that benefits everyone. Most importantly, individuals saw themselves as active participants in their health journeys, equipped with personalized tools and resources to make lasting lifestyle changes. By framing Newtopia's future vision as a collective effort, Jeff successfully created a shared narrative that inspires action and commitment from all stakeholders.

To create a shared future, ask yourself: How can others be part of your vision? What role do your customers, employees, and partners play in making this future a reality? A shared Future Narrative works best when it provides clear ways for others to engage—when it empowers people to take meaningful actions that contribute to the bigger picture. This could mean inviting customers to be co-creators, allowing employees to take ownership of projects that align with the vision, or forging partnerships that multiply the impact of your future vision.

A shared future should feel inclusive. It must make people feel valued, appreciated, and vital to the success of the vision. People feel a sense of belonging and pride when they understand how their actions contribute to a broader purpose. For customers, it means they aren't just buying a product or service—they're contributing to something that aligns with their values. For employees, it means their work is more than just a job; it's a part of something transformative. For partners and collaborators, it's about aligning with a cause representing meaningful change.

The power of a shared future lies in its ability to unite people around a common purpose. It turns a Future Narrative from an individual vision into a collective mission, where everyone involved feels empowered to contribute. By inviting others to share in the journey, you not only broaden the reach of your vision but also create a committed community ready to make that future a reality.

Preparing for Strategic Action

Crafting a Future Narrative is an ambitious endeavour that defines your company's future and how you shape your industry. By defining a powerful future vision, crafting a strategic story that brings it to life, making it deeply personal, and creating a shared future, you position yourself as a true leader—a visionary capable of inspiring transformation on a large scale. However, a future narrative is just the beginning; the next step is to turn this narrative into strategic action that translates your vision into real-world impact.

The journey doesn't end with a compelling story—it starts there. Yvon Chouinard's commitment to sustainability turned Patagonia into a symbol of environmental advocacy, proving that businesses can lead the charge in protecting the planet. Jeff Ruby's vision for preventative healthcare reimagined an industry traditionally focused on treatment, shifting the focus to proactive wellness through personalized programs. Victoria Lennox's dedication to empowering entrepreneurs transformed Canada's startup ecosystem, ensuring that grassroots founders had the resources, networks, and advocacy needed to succeed. These leaders turned their Future Narratives into action, creating movements that reshaped their industries.

As you move forward, consider the actions needed to support your Future Narrative. How will you bring your strategic story to life day by day? What steps will ensure that your personal narrative resonates not only in words but also in actions? And how can you ensure that others feel engaged and inspired to contribute to this shared future? This means aligning your operations, goals, and culture with your narrative, making every part of your company a reflection of your vision.

The power of a Future Narrative lies in its ability to mobilize and inspire. It's about taking your future vision and translating it into something others can see, understand, and rally around. As you craft your Future Narrative, let it be a living, dynamic story that grows with your company—one that not only tells people where you're headed but also brings them along on the journey.

The challenge now is to take the bold ideas you've outlined and transform them into actions that embody the story you've told. Remember, a Future Narrative is most powerful when it is realized through consistent and purposeful action. This is your opportunity to take the lead, to not just imagine the future but to actively shape it and inspire others to do the same.

Chapter 3 will guide you through the principles of Category Evangelization, focusing on how to amplify your Future Narrative across platforms, build momentum, and create an industry-defining movement. Let's move from crafting a story to actively spreading and amplifying it, ensuring your vision gains the traction and impact it deserves.

Crafting Your Future Narrative
Download the Chapter Worksheet

Structure and craft your Future Narrative with this guided worksheet.

resources.futurenarrator.com/narrative

CHAPTER 3

Category Evangelization – Turning a Vision into a Movement

From Vision to Movement

Do you have a vision that could change the game in your industry? Maybe it's stuck in your head or buried in a slide deck. What separates bold leaders is their ability to transform that vision into a movement that inspires action. Having a Future Narrative isn't just about defining a vision—it's about ensuring that vision spreads, gains momentum, and takes on a life of its own. These leaders use evangelization to bring it to life by rallying teams, engaging communities, and positioning themselves as the driving force behind industry change.

I saw this firsthand when I attended Dan Martell's book launch in Toronto. Dan didn't just write his bestselling book, *Buy Back Your Time*—he built a movement around it. Through SaaS Academy, live events, and a relentless focus on sharing his message across platforms, Dan has created a global community of SaaS founders who follow his methods and evangelize them. Watching how he engages his audience, amplifies his message, and aligns his team to seamlessly produce and distribute content inspired me to take evangelization more seriously.

Evangelization is making your Future Narrative the defining story in your industry. Throughout this chapter, I'll share insights from two leaders I interviewed on my podcast, who have both taken impressive steps to evangelize a Future Narrative: Mark Organ, a pioneer in customer advocacy and category creation, and Cherry Rose Tan, a leader in mental health for tech founders, who has successfully leveraged community engagement to amplify her vision. Their journeys offer invaluable lessons in how to take an idea from a personal vision to an industry-defining movement.

Evangelizing a Future Narrative requires a strategic approach to making your message resonate and take hold in your industry. This chapter explores The Pillars of Evangelization—Consistency, Strategy, and Amplification—as the foundation for ensuring your message is clear, relevant, and widely shared. We'll then discuss Internal Evangelization and how embedding your Future Narrative within your organization turns employees into its strongest advocates. From there, we'll cover Amplifying the Message through media and partnerships, Engaging Early Adopters to refine and validate the narrative, and Evangelizing Through Community to build long-term advocacy. Finally, we'll examine Evangelization as a Continuous Journey, emphasizing the importance of resilience, feedback, and adaptation to keep your Future Narrative strong and relevant.

This chapter will guide you through these critical elements, providing actionable strategies to ensure your Future Narrative doesn't just exist—it thrives. Now, let's begin with the Pillars of Evangelization.

The Pillars of Evangelization - Consistency, Strategy, and Amplification

To transform a vision into a movement, leaders must rely on three key pillars: Consistency, Strategy, and Amplification. These pillars work together as interdependent components, supporting the ongoing process of bringing a Future Narrative to life.

Consistency: Building Trust and Credibility

The first pillar, consistency, is about becoming known for your point of view (POV) and making your Future Narrative a story that people not only hear repeatedly but also adopt as their own. Consistently sharing your vision ensures that others see the present world as old news and recognize the future world you're building as where it's at. When your message is clear, persistent, and aligned with your values, it becomes the foundation for trust and credibility, creating advocates who champion your vision.

When Mark Organ was on my show, he stood out as one of the most skilled at bringing people on board with a Future Narrative. Through his work at Eloqua and Influitive, he consistently communicated the value of customer advocacy and built systems that delivered measurable results. His dedication to showcasing success stories—like how personalized onboarding led to faster adoption—helped him turn clients into advocates who actively championed his vision. Mark's example shows how consistency creates a ripple effect, embedding your narrative in the minds of others and building a loyal, trusting community.

Strategy: Tailoring the Message for Different Audiences

The second pillar, strategy, requires adapting the message for different audiences while preserving the core vision. When I went to Dan Martell's book signing, he did a small talk about going pro by treating content creation like running a media company—going hard and being systematic on social media. That was the moment that lit a fire for me, and I decided to take social media marketing seriously. I developed a strategy and consistently put out content, testing responses and tweaking it as I went. The entire year of the Future Narrator Project has been one of trial and error— putting out the message, gathering feedback, and iterating. This approach is now central to how we operate: adapt the message to the response, refine it, and move forward.

Mark Organ really impacted me with how adaptive he was with his messaging. On my podcast, he shared how he tailored his message to resonate with both SaaS founders and enterprise executives. Through platforms like Influitive's AdvocateHub, he crafted narratives that highlighted the specific benefits of customer advocacy for each audience. By aligning his message with the unique needs of his stakeholders, Mark ensured his vision was both practical and inspiring, driving engagement across diverse sectors.

Amplification: Expanding Reach and Creating Impact

The third pillar, amplification, ensures that the Future Narrative reaches beyond its initial circle. With the launch of our book, we've been tackling this pillar head-on. Collision Conference in Toronto was a key opportunity to get in front of industry leaders and collaborate with them to leverage our networks. It also helped lay the groundwork for building relationships with the organizers. The conference was the perfect venue for interacting with our avatars and getting their feedback, and this book is the result of multitudes of interactions with our community. We can replicate this approach with other communities now that we've tested the waters and built a proof of concept.

Now that our podcast and book demonstrate our process in action, we have moved to targeted outreach for speaking engagements. Paul's experience working with leaders as a TEDx coach and speech writer allows us to tailor our future narrative and stories to the specific needs of each community. There are so many opportunities for collaboration and partnerships to amplify our message.

My interview with Mark Organ inspired the development of our process. Long before Paul and I began creating the Future Narrator project, he was my role model for how amplification can transform a Future Narrative into a movement. He leveraged media, conferences, and customer advocacy programs to amplify the message of customer-led growth. Through keynote speeches, he positioned Influitive as the go-to solution for businesses looking to scale through advocacy. His amplification efforts turned his Future Narrative into a recognized movement, establishing Influitive as a leader in advocate marketing.

Consistency, strategy, and amplification are like the gears of a finely tuned machine—they work together seamlessly to bring your Future Narrative to life. Consistency builds trust by ensuring your message is always present and recognizable. Strategy keeps the message relevant, adapting it to meet the needs of different audiences. Amplification takes that message further, extending your reach and making a lasting impact. Together, they create the foundation for a powerful and sustainable movement. Now, we can begin evangelizing internally to our team and externally to our community.

Internal Evangelization - Creating Buy-In Through Your Future Narrative

Before a Future Narrative can make an external impact, it must first take root within the organization. Internal evangelization is about rallying employee support to bring the narrative to life. Aligned teams embody the Future Narrative daily, with each employee feeling personally connected to its success.

Paul has extensive experience in writing employment brand stories for companies, taking their vision and mission and making it deeply meaningful to employees and candidates. Employment branding focuses on creating buy-in to the company vision by articulating its purpose and aligning it with individual roles. But a Future Narrative takes this a step further—it transforms the leader's vision of the future, their story of where they're going, and their unique point of view into a movement. With a Future Narrative, the employment brand becomes part of a unifying story that inspires employees, candidates, and stakeholders to rally around a shared purpose. When employees understand how their work contributes to a larger vision, they become passionate advocates.

When Paul is called in to help companies struggling with recruitment, he often finds their vision and mission falling flat—buried somewhere on the website, with no real meaning to employees or candidates. His process begins with deep discussions with the CEO, uncovering their vision for the company and why it matters to them. He looks for personal stories and defining moments that reveal the leader's purpose and drive, breathing life into the vision and mission. From there, he conducts interviews and focus groups with employees to understand their experiences and perceptions of the company culture. By weaving the employee experience into the leader's story and vision, he creates a narrative people can relate to and see themselves in. This turns the Future Narrative into a shared story that fosters personal growth while driving the company's success.

Building an Internal Evangelization Strategy

An effective internal evangelization strategy relies on ongoing communication, active listening, and celebrating successes. Leaders should keep the vision alive through multiple channels, such as email updates, team meetings, and workshops. Listening to feedback and adjusting accordingly fosters collaboration and shared ownership. This helps employees feel part of something bigger, turning them into powerful ambassadors who help drive the movement beyond the organization.

External Evangelization - Leveraging Media, Events, and Partnerships

External evangelization is the bridge between a compelling Future Narrative and a movement that inspires action. Once internal buy-in is established, the focus shifts to extending the narrative's reach through three powerful avenues: media, live events, and strategic partnerships. Each plays a vital role in making your Future Narrative resonate beyond the walls of your organization.

Media Engagement: Telling Your Story Consistently

One of the most effective ways to amplify your narrative is through media. This means identifying key platforms like podcasts, industry publications, and social media where your audience spends time. The goal is to show up consistently, reinforcing your story with every appearance.

Media provides an unparalleled opportunity to share your point of view, not just as a one-time event but as an ongoing dialogue. When you commit to consistent storytelling, your message becomes familiar, accessible, and, most importantly, credible. Every article, interview, or post should echo the central themes of your Future Narrative, helping others see the world through your lens and adopt your vision as their own.

Live Events: Creating Real-Time Connections

Live events are where the narrative comes alive. Whether it's conferences, workshops, or industry panels, these events allow you to directly engage with your audience in meaningful ways. The beauty of live events lies in their immediacy—they create shared experiences that leave lasting impressions.

At these gatherings, you have the chance to articulate your vision, spark conversations, and build genuine connections. It's not just about being present; it's about being memorable. These moments of clarity and interaction amplify your message far beyond the event itself, creating ripple effects that carry your narrative to new audiences.

Strategic Partnerships: Expanding Your Influence

The third avenue of external evangelization is strategic partnerships. By collaborating with influential players who share your values or complement your vision, you can multiply the impact of your message. Partnerships provide access to new networks and amplify credibility, helping your narrative reach people you might not connect with otherwise.

Strategic partnerships could involve co-hosted events, joint ventures, or endorsements. The key is ensuring these collaborations align with your Future Narrative, strengthening the story you're telling and extending its reach.

When I interviewed Mark Organ, his mastery of external evangelization stood out. Since that conversation, I've followed his journey and been continually impressed by his use of these three pillars. Mark uses media to share his vision of customer advocacy, regularly appearing on podcasts and in articles reinforcing his message. His presence at live events, like the Crowdsourcing Week (CSW) Summit, makes an impact in real-time, engaging audiences with compelling stories that inspire action. His ability to forge strategic partnership has been so successful that other companies now seek his guidance to replicate his approach.

External evangelization is about transforming the landscape of your industry by strategically leveraging media, live events, and partnerships. This is not something you can do alone. With a team aligned through a strong Future Narrative, they can take everything you say and do and turn it into powerfully aligned content for your amplification plan.

Audience Engagement: Listening and Iterating

Engaging with your community is essential for amplifying and refining your Future Narrative. I regularly track how Dan Martell goes pro with his social media presence. He consistently interacts with his community and shares content perfectly aligned with his Future Narrative, showing up in a way that resonates deeply with his audience.

What stands about Dan's approach wis how aligned his team is with his message. He has two camera angles on his desk recording him at all times—whether he's doing a talk, a coaching call, or just working. His team takes anything of value he says and turns it into curated content for the right platform. They know his future narrative and how he shows up, so every content piece perfectly reflects his brand and movement. That level of alignment is what makes his content resonate so effectively.

Our experience at Collision Conference is another example of interaction and iteration in action. The interviews we did at the event became podcast episodes. Still, more importantly, we were engaging with the community, gathering insights, and refining our messaging to create the content for this book. Over the year, I've shared content with our community, interacted with early adopters, and used their feedback to fine-tune our messaging. Every iteration has brought us more resonance with our audience and built a narrative that feels like it belongs to them.

Engaging early adopters starts with listening. Leaders should seek feedback to understand what works and what needs improvement. By valuing their input, early adopters become partners in the journey because they see the potential to solve meaningful problems. Through personal connections, early adopters can become active advocates. They also value recognition through exclusive events or case studies. Listening to early adopters, involving them in the narrative, and providing platforms for them to share their experiences create a ripple effect. Their stories inspire others to join the movement, driving the momentum of your Future Narrative.

Evangelizing Through Community

After engaging early adopters, the next step is to harness the power of community to propel the movement forward. Community-building fosters belonging connects individuals to the Future Narrative, and amplifies the message.

My friend Cherry Rose Tan, who successfully launched her own book, Still Standing: What It Takes to Thrive and Innovate in a Messy World, is an inspiring example of leveraging community through live events and content. Her book launch drew an impressive turnout of influential individuals from her community, all united by the shared energy and purpose around her message. Seeing how effectively she engaged her community underscored the power of deep, authentic connections in building a movement.

A strong community is essential for amplifying a Future Narrative. It turns individual supporters into a cohesive movement. Building a community starts by creating spaces where people can connect and share, such as online forums, social media, or exclusive platforms. Leaders should prioritize creating a sense of collective belonging, helping participants feel they are part of something greater than themselves.

Influencers who share your vision can significantly amplify the Future Narrative. Leaders should identify key figures in their industry who align with their vision and collaborate through workshops, interviews, or joint events to draw new participants and grow the movement. For this book, I'm leaning heavily on my own community to help amplify our message. From sharing early content to providing feedback, they've been instrumental in shaping the narrative and creating outreach opportunities. This collaborative effort ensures our Future Narrative reflects the collective energy and purpose of everyone involved.

Sustaining engagement requires ongoing effort. A strong Future Narrative your team understands and is aligned with makes it much easier to create content that resonates with the community and encourages active participation. Leaders should provide opportunities for continued involvement, such as regular updates, exclusive content, or follow-up events. Tools like social media groups, newsletters, and webinars help keep the community connected between events, ensuring members remain informed, inspired, and committed.

Effective community-building elevates an idea into an enduring movement. Consider how you can harness the power of community to drive your Future Narrative. How can you create shared experiences that deepen connections? Who are the influencers that can help you extend your reach? By focusing on community, you can create an environment where your Future Narrative thrives.

Evangelization as a Continuous Journey

Evangelizing a Future Narrative is an ongoing journey requiring continuous effort, adaptation, and resilience. Over the past year, I've experienced firsthand what it means to adapt and refine our Future Narrative. It hasn't always been easy, but it has been necessary.

Getting feedback can be tough. At times, it's meant putting egos aside and choosing to be grateful that our community is willing to share what they want to hear about and how our material impacts— or doesn't land. One of the key things I've worked on is playing with the consistency of our posting across different platforms. I've studied the responses, and consistency is paying off. It's generating engagement from our advocates and shaping the community, clarifying who wants to be a part of it.

Of course, this journey hasn't been without rejection. We've had to make significant changes to the content of our book based on the feedback and reactions we've received. Some people didn't feel like they were part of the journey, and that's something we've worked hard to address. Still, we keep engaging, shaping our message, and getting closer to the mark in an iterative process. Every adjustment makes our narrative stronger and more resonant.

This engagement and interaction aren't just about refining the narrative—they're also generating valuable leads and connections. One thing is certain: I'm much happier with how the book reflects us now. Our message is clearer, stronger, and resonates more deeply with people. They get it without us needing to explain it, which is a huge win.

Engagement with the community and iteration is hard but deeply gratifying when you commit to the process and move past the fear of rejection. It's the effort and resilience in this ongoing journey that make the Future Narrative truly powerful and impactful.

From Thought Leadership to Category Ownership

Evangelizing a Future Narrative is about transforming a bold idea into a movement that inspires action but it starts where you are today. Once you have a working version of your Future Narrative vision, you must invite others to join you. Engaging with your community creates a shared sense of purpose and momentum that turns ideas into tangible change. Throughout this chapter, we've explored achieving category ownership by aligning your team, amplifying your message, engaging early adopters, and fostering a supportive community.

Category ownership is built on the foundation of a community that believes in your vision and is willing to help carry it forward. Reflecting on this journey, I'm reminded of the importance of resilience, consistency, and adaptability. These qualities have guided our efforts to refine and share our Future Narrative, and they're essential for anyone looking to lead a movement that leaves a lasting impact.

Engaging early adopters, listening to their feedback, and iterating on your message is challenging but rewarding. Through this process of interaction and adaptation, your narrative gains strength and clarity, resonating more deeply with your community. A strong Future Narrative creates alignment within your team and builds trust and loyalty among stakeholders, making it easier for advocates to spread the message.

In the next chapter, we'll explore how podcasting can play a pivotal role in evangelizing your Future Narrative. By sharing insightful conversations and creating memorable sound bites, podcasting allows you to reach new audiences, deepen engagement, and refine your message in real-time. It's another powerful tool to add to your evangelization strategy.

Evangelizing Your Future Narrative
Download the Chapter Worksheet

Use this worksheet to build momentum and share your vision effectively.

resources.futurenarrator.com/movement

CHAPTER 4

The Power of the Podcast

Podcasting as a Tool for Clarity and Communication

Imagine having a platform where you can refine your thoughts, reach an audience, and build your credibility all at once. Podcasting offers exactly that—a powerful medium for sharing your message and actively sharpening it. As a thought leader, your journey requires you to communicate effectively and develop your voice in real-time. Podcasting transforms raw ideas into refined narratives that resonate deeply with listeners, helping you articulate a vision that can lead an industry.

Building on the concepts discussed in Chapter 3, where we explored evangelizing the Future Narrative, podcasting is one of the most effective mediums to actively refine and spread that narrative. It's a medium for reaching your audience, developing yourself as a communicator, and ensuring that your story resonates in its most impactful form.

To demonstrate the power of podcasting, we will explore the approaches of two renowned podcasters—Peter Diamandis and Gary Vaynerchuk (GaryVee). Additionally, I'll share the experience of successful founder Shrad Rao, CEO of Wagepoint, whom I've had the privilege of interviewing on my own podcast. Shrad used a podcast tour to connect with audiences, amplify his message, and build credibility, later launching his own podcast to further leverage this medium. Finally, we'll examine the inspiring journey of Vicky Saunders, founder of SheEO, who not only hosts her own podcast but also appears as a guest on others, using this platform to expand her reach, build community, and inspire action through radical generosity.

Podcasting is unique in its intimacy and accessibility. Unlike other forms of content, podcasts allow listeners to engage deeply with your ideas—often during personal moments, such as commuting or exercising. This creates an opportunity for thought leaders to build trust, nurture a community, and inspire listeners through authentic conversations.

For those seeking category ownership, podcasting can be the first step in transforming a broad vision into a cohesive, shareable narrative. The process of discussing your ideas, hearing yourself articulate a Future Narrative, and refining that message is invaluable in shaping thought leadership.

The Benefits of Recording

Recording a podcast requires you to bring clarity to your thoughts. Unlike casual conversations, recording makes you acutely aware of your audience and the need to communicate effectively. This shift in mindset encourages you to be deliberate in choosing your words, structuring your ideas, and ensuring that your message is clear. As you hear yourself speak, you become more adept at identifying areas that need refinement, ultimately helping you develop sound bites and key phrases that effectively communicate your vision.

Throughout our collaboration, Paul and I decided that to up our game, we would record every one of our conversations. This was easy enough on our video calls, but we took it further. As a podcaster and gear nerd, I got a set of wireless lapel mics that we wear for our in-person conversation. I also use these for impromptu on-site interviews. We have transcripts of all our conversations and some of the valuable information captured has become part of this book.

Peter Diamandis shows how recording can turn bold, complex ideas into clear, inspiring stories anyone can connect with. With his focus on the future of technology and human longevity, he uses podcasting as a dynamic tool to simplify and refine big concepts, making them relatable to a broad audience. Through his Moonshot Podcast, Peter articulates his vision and engages deeply with influential guests like Ray Dalio and Steven Kotler. These high-profile conversations explore economic trends, flow science, and the future of human potential, adding new dimensions to his discussions. By bringing in experts from different fields, Peter not only elevates his credibility but also expands the scope of his message, ensuring it resonates across industries. These conversations are thought-provoking explorations that sharpen his thinking and deepen the impact of his ideas. For founders, recording can work the same way—helping them refine their message, test their ideas in real-world conversations, and turn ambitious thoughts into compelling narratives that truly connect with their audience.

Podcasting creates a powerful feedback loop. Each recording lets you see what resonates and needs work, refining your Future Narrative. Recording gives you the space to practice and evolve your story so you're ready to share it clearly and confidently in interviews, live events, or other opportunities.

Developing Multipurpose Content

Podcasting is a fantastic way of reaching people directly and offers endless possibilities to repurpose your content. Every episode you record becomes raw material for social media posts, quote cards, audiograms—you name it. A single podcast can stretch across platforms, giving your message more reach and impact.

GaryVee is a master at this. His approach to repurposing content is legendary. He calls podcast episodes "pillar content" because they are the foundation for everything else. One episode might turn into a series of tweets, a LinkedIn post, an Instagram reel, and even a YouTube clip. This way, he ensures his core message reaches people in different formats and on platforms where they're already active. It's an incredible way to amplify impact and stay consistent.

Another clever approach is creating miniseries. You can group episodes around specific themes to dive deep into your Future Narrative. This helps you organize your content and gives your audience a clear and structured way to follow along. It's like offering them a guided journey through your ideas.

Repurposing content is about making every recording count. GaryVee's strategy of breaking down long-form content into bite-sized, platform-friendly pieces is something any founder can adopt. On top of extending your message's life span, you make sure it connects with people wherever they are.

What I love about podcasting is its versatility. It's a content goldmine that builds momentum for your Future Narrative and reinforces your thought leadership. Every recording has the potential to become something much bigger, reaching people in ways you might not have imagined at first.

Leveraging Guest Appearances to Mobilize Thought Leadership

One of the most effective ways to begin your podcasting journey is by appearing as a guest on other podcasts. For example, Shrad Rao strategically used a podcast tour to connect with diverse audiences, amplify his message, and build credibility as a thought leader. When I had Shrad on my podcast, it was clear how intentional he was about sharing his story. He wasn't just explaining the success of Wagepoint; he was crafting a narrative about culture, leadership, and innovation. His tour exposed him to different audiences and allowed him to refine his messaging based on real-time feedback. After seeing the impact, Shrad eventually launched his own podcast to expand his reach further and maximize the benefits of this medium.

Appearing on podcasts as a guest not only positions you as an expert in your field but also helps build connections with other thought leaders. It's a chance to collaborate, share ideas, and introduce your audience to new perspectives while benefiting from the credibility of the podcast host.

Hosting your own podcast takes your thought leadership to the next level. By creating a platform for conversations with other leaders, you build credibility through association and develop content that extends far beyond the initial recording. I've experienced this firsthand, particularly during our work at the Collision Conference in Toronto.

At Collision, Paul and I decided to use podcasting to position ourselves as experts in cultivating leadership and building future narratives. With media access, we interviewed 21 thought leaders over three days, creating a wealth of content that inspired our listeners and laid the foundation for this book. These 20-minute interviews became podcast episodes, social media content, audiograms, and profiles that you will find at the end of this book. The process demonstrates the power of podcasting in action to generate multipurpose content and solidify credibility.

Podcasting, whether as a guest or a host, is a powerful way to amplify your message, build credibility, and inspire action. As a guest, you leverage established platforms to share your story and reach new audiences. As a host, you take control of the narrative, creating a space for meaningful conversations that reinforce your expertise and connect you with other leaders.

Establishing Credibility and Thought Leadership

When I interviewed Vicki Saunders on my podcast, I could feel her passion for creating change. As the founder of SheEO, Vicki is on a mission to transform how we support female entrepreneurs, and her concept of "radical generosity" is nothing short of revolutionary. What struck me most during our conversation was how she used podcasting—not just hers, but also as a guest on others' shows—to amplify her mission and build a movement.

Vicki shared stories about how SheEO works, from gathering hundreds of women as activators to pooling their contributions into a fund that supports female-led ventures. But what stood out was the way she framed everything. Her storytelling invited people into her vision. She could share authentic stories of impact through her podcasting efforts, like how one entrepreneur saw 500% revenue growth after joining the network—proof of what's possible when you rethink how we fund and support innovation.

Vicki leverages the power of podcasting by inviting others into the conversation. On her own podcast and as a guest, she brings in voices from all over—activators, entrepreneurs, advocates—and creates an inclusive and inspiring dialogue. When I listened to her explain how SheEO gives every entrepreneur in their network instant access to 500 supporters, it clicked: her success isn't just about the money but the community she's building.

Something else I've learned from Vicki is how podcasting helps you solidify your message. SheEO's core ideas—like "radical generosity"—have become synonymous with her brand because she repeats them consistently across every platform. Vicki has since rebranded as Coralus but when people hear "radical generosity," they know exactly what she stands for, and that clarity builds trust.

My conversation with Vicki reminded me why I started podcasting in the first place: to connect, inspire, and build something bigger than myself. Through her appearances on podcasts and on her podcast, Vicki shows us how to use our voices to spark change and mobilize others to join us.

The Power of Podcasting to Accelerate Thought Leadership

Podcasting is a game-changer for thought leadership. Whether refining your message, connecting with your audience, or building credibility, podcasting can amplify your voice and mobilize your ideas in ways other platforms can't match.

It's easy to look at big names like Peter Diamandis and GaryVee and think, "That works for them because they're already successful," but podcasting works for anyone willing to put themselves out there. Shrad Rao didn't start out as a household name. Still, by leveraging a podcast tour and launching his own podcast, he refined his story, expanded his reach, and positioned himself as a leader in payroll innovation.

Vicki Saunders used podcasting to share the story of SheEO and build a community around her vision of radical generosity. Hosting her own podcast and appearing as a guest on others has allowed her to connect with people who resonate with her message and want to be part of her mission.

The beauty of podcasting is that it's a tool anyone can use to amplify their thought leadership. Whether you're sharing actionable tips like GaryVee, diving into big ideas like Peter Diamandis, or building movements like Shrad and Vicki, podcasting gives you the platform to make your voice heard and inspire others.

In the next chapter, we'll explore how to turn your content— whether through podcasting, blogs, or other mediums—into something more permanent and impactful, like a book. Just as podcasting helps you articulate your Future Narrative, a book allows you to solidify it, ensuring your ideas live on and continue to influence others. In the next chapter we'll dive in and explore how to make that happen.

Podcasting as a Thought Leadership Tool
Download the Chapter Worksheet

Plan and launch your podcast using this step-by-step worksheet.
resources.futurenarrator.com/podcast

CHAPTER 5

Legacy Through Content - From Podcast to Book

Imagine a world where your ideas don't just reach people—they change how they think. That's exactly what Tim Ferriss did with his experiments and insights. The launch of his book, 'The 4-Hour Workweek,' transformed the narrative he'd been refining for years into a movement. He turned his content into a legacy, establishing himself as a thought leader and reshaping how millions view work and life. What if your Future Narrative could do the same?

In the last chapter, we explored how iterative storytelling and the power of podcasts can amplify your Future Narrative, building credibility and resonance. Now, we'll take it a step further, showing how these efforts culminate in creating legacy content that establishes your authority and ensures that your influence endures for years. This chapter focuses on the final stage of the Future Narrator Framework, where all the raw data and iterative content are transformed into legacy assets like a podcast miniseries and a book.

In the sections ahead, we'll delve into how refining and amplifying your Future Narrative lays the groundwork for legacy content, the role podcasting plays as a foundation, and the importance of iterative storytelling. We'll explore how this process leads to creating books and podcast miniseries and how to amplify these assets to solidify your authority and expand your influence.

I've had the privilege of interviewing two incredible guests on my podcast who embody this transformative process. Cherry Rose Tan, who we first met in Chapter 3, is a trailblazer in mental health leadership and uses her platform to refine and amplify her vision, turning raw insights into impactful narratives. Liam Martin, a remote work and productivity pioneer, demonstrates how strategic content creation and podcasting can evolve into enduring assets that shape industries. Their journeys provide a roadmap for creating your own legacy content.

The Power of a Well-Crafted Narrative

A successful book is founded on a well-crafted narrative—developed, refined, and shaped by putting your message out there, testing it, and adapting it to your audience. This process is personal and iterative. When we pre-released a C+ version of our book to our community, we were blown away by the support we received. We asked for unapologetic feedback, and in some cases, that's exactly what we got. This experience refined our narrative and pushed us to include more personal stories and examples to make it our own. Pulling insights from my podcast episodes, I was amazed at the incredible business leaders I had interviewed—each story adding depth and perspective. Sharing the learning along the way helped us refine our message and brought valuable lessons to our readers. Every podcast episode, interview, and social post builds a narrative that resonates authentically with your audience and makes your message unforgettable.

Tim Ferriss built his reputation by consistently sharing experiments and insights across multiple channels—blogs, podcasts, and public talks—strengthening an engaging and coherent narrative. His focus on breaking free from traditional work structures and designing a life centred around freedom, efficiency, and personal fulfillment was apparent in everything he shared. "The Tim Ferriss Show" became a pivotal platform for refining these ideas, as he used interviews with experts to explore topics like optimizing workflows, mastering health habits, and redefining success. Conversations with thought leaders like Derek Sivers and Dr. Peter Attia helped him hone concepts of productivity and well-being, reinforcing his central theme that unconventional thinking can lead to extraordinary results. This iterative and multi-platform development enhanced his credibility and laid the groundwork for his book, 'The 4-Hour Workweek,' turning it into a cornerstone of his thought leadership.

Revisiting past content through the lens of your Future Narrative can transform how you see your work and its impact. When we began looking back at my podcast episodes and interviews with this perspective, it gave us a completely different view of what my guests were sharing and how their insights strengthened our Future Narrative. Writing a book forces you into this comprehensive reflection. It reveals gaps, inconsistencies, and the variety in your content that might not be obvious in standalone pieces like podcast episodes.

For us, the writing process showed how vital it was to find a unifying thread—the central story that ties everything together. That thread is your Future Narrative. Starting with it makes each podcast episode or content more impactful because your audience senses the alignment. This alignment keeps them returning, strengthens connections with the right people, and pulls your community together. The legacy pieces that result—a book and a podcast miniseries—become the anchors for your strategic narrative and the cornerstones of your thought leadership.

Leveraging Podcasts to Develop the Book

Podcasting offers a rich source of content that can serve as the foundation of a book. Each episode, interview, or conversation contributes to building a broader narrative. Podcast content allows you to expand on resonant ideas, explore topics in-depth, and create a structured progression that aligns with your vision.

Tim Ferriss used 'The Tim Ferriss Show' as a testing ground for ideas that eventually formed the backbone of his books. He featured a diverse lineup of guests—from athletes like Arnold Schwarzenegger to entrepreneurs like Reid Hoffman—creating a platform for in-depth discussions on productivity, lifestyle design, and more. These conversations enabled Ferriss to explore themes of productivity, lifestyle design, and personal growth, identifying what resonated most with his audience. For instance, many interviews focused on the routines and habits of high achievers, which became central themes in his books like The *4-Hour Workweek and Tools of Titans.*

Podcasting's iterative nature is invaluable for developing book content. Each episode offers a chance to explore themes from different angles, respond to audience feedback, and refine ideas. This process sharpens your message and ensures the material is tested and validated by your audience before it becomes part of your book. Ferriss regularly incorporated listener feedback, identifying which concepts resonated and where further elaboration was needed. This iterative approach ensured his books aligned well with his audience's interests and needs.

Case studies of successful thought leaders transitioning from podcast to book illustrate the power of this approach. This book provides a real-time example: the 21 thought leaders interviewed from Collision Conference are now featured here, turning their insights into a lasting legacy. These thought leaders not only share their expertise but also provide examples and stories throughout the book, enhancing reader engagement. Additionally, we have included QR codes that direct readers to specific thought leader podcast episodes, effectively bridging the gap between the podcast and the book and allowing readers to dig deeper into the topics discussed.

By leveraging podcast content to develop your book, you ensure that your ideas are refined, tested, and validated. This approach makes the book writing process more efficient and ensures the final product deeply connects with your audience's interests and needs. Podcasting helps uncover the core of your message while the book presents that message in its most complete and impactful form.

Building Authority with Your Book Launch

Marketing is critical. Launching a book doesn't start on publication day—it begins long before it is finished. People must follow you, invest in your ideas, and engage in the process as you write it. That's why I decided to go pro with social media this year. Sharing about the book-writing journey on the platforms where I wanted to connect with my audience wasn't just about visibility but building a relationship. I practicing what I preach: creating a narrative that people can follow and feel part of, even before they turn the first page.

When it comes to leveraging PR and networks effectively, I think of my friend and colleague, Cherry Rose Tan. She did an incredible job during her book launch for *Still Standing*. She used her network and PR strategies to bring people to her launch events and secure media coverage that amplified her message. Her book became a conversation starter across platforms, and she engaged her audience with authenticity and intention. Cherry Rose's efforts show how important it is to align your launch with your larger strategic goals while making it personal and engaging.

PR campaigns are essential to establishing credibility and ensuring your book launch doesn't go unnoticed. Without an audience, it's like throwing a message in a bottle into the ocean. You might hope it reaches someone, but there's no guarantee. PR builds anticipation, positioning you as an expert and creating the buzz to excite people. Media coverage, interviews, and press releases help amplify your message, and showing up in respected publications or high-profile platforms adds weight to your authority.

Strategic PR ensures your book reaches the right audience—those who can benefit from and amplify your content. That's why planning your launch starts long before the book is finished. Take it from Tim Ferriss and Dan Martell, who recognized the power of sharing their books early, sending drafts to the right people, and asking for feedback. They built anticipation by involving their audience in the process, making the final product feel like a shared success.

I've learned much from their examples, and their influence has shaped my social media strategy over the past year. It's been a learning curve, but I've been getting comfortable engaging with the platforms where I want to connect with my audience. Asking for feedback can be daunting, too, but taking a step back and seeing it from your community's point of view is priceless. It keeps them engaged, and they tell you what they want to hear. Sharing the process creates anticipation and builds relationships that excite people to support the launch.

Make the goal of writing a book about the process rather than the end result. Waiting until you have the book in hand is too late. When the process is shared strategically, it can open doors to speaking stages, interviews, and media coverage that amplify your message far beyond its pages. Planning for this reach and visibility ensures the book resonates with the people who matter most and positions you as a definitive voice in your field. The sooner you start weaving this into your strategy, the more impactful your launch will be.

Creating a Long-Term Impact: Beyond the Book Launch

Publishing a book is a big deal, but as Liam Martin proved with *Running Remote: Master the Lessons from the World's Most Successful Remote-Work Pioneers*, it's just the beginning of the journey. A book's real power isn't just in its launch day hype—it's in how its message continues to resonate and evolve long after it hits the shelves. If you want your book to have a lasting impact, you must think beyond the launch and plan for what comes next.

A book is your foundation, your springboard. But keeping that momentum alive takes work. Liam turned *Running Remote* into the centrepiece of ongoing conversations through his conferences, podcasts, and speaking engagements. He used these platforms to build on the book's themes, engage directly with his audience, and keep the narrative growing. The key here is consistency. When you share insights through talks, podcast episodes, articles, or even social media, you keep the story alive and reach new audiences every time.

Think about how much more powerful your message can become when amplified across platforms. A chapter of your book can become a keynote speech, a podcast series, or a viral LinkedIn post. Each format gives you a new way to connect with your audience and ensures your message reaches people wherever they are. By repurposing your content, you're not just expanding your reach but maximizing the impact of every idea you've shared.

But it's not just about broadcasting—it's about connecting. Engaging your audience after the launch means inviting them into the conversation. Liam fostered honest dialogue around remote work by creating spaces for feedback and interaction through his *Running Remote conference* and *The Future Workforce Podcast*. Hosting Q&A sessions, webinars, and online discussions keeps the ideas fresh and relevant, making your audience feel part of something bigger.

A book is an incredible legacy, but ongoing engagement solidifies your thought leadership. The narrative doesn't end when your book is published—that's just the first chapter. As you interact with your audience, refine your ideas, and share your vision, your message gains depth and staying power. The long-term strategy takes your ideas from a one-time launch to lasting influence, ensuring you're shaping your industry for years.

Expanding Reach Through Multimedia Content

Integrating multimedia content into the promotion and post-launch phases significantly extends a book's reach. Leveraging different forms of media ensures your content is accessible to a wider audience, allowing your book's message to resonate with diverse learners and consumers.

Video Content, like book trailers or short clips, creates buzz and captures the attention of audiences who prefer visual formats. Tim Ferriss used YouTube to share concise, engaging clips summarizing key lessons from 'The 4-Hour Workweek,' generating excitement and extending content relevance. A well-crafted book trailer highlights key themes and sparks interest, while video content shared on social media broadens your reach.

Audiobooks make your content accessible to those who prefer listening. Tim Ferriss's audiobook version of 'The 4-Hour Workweek' reached a mobile audience, expanding the accessibility of his ideas. Audiobooks cater to people learning during commutes, workouts, or other activities, ensuring your message reaches those without time to read. They also convey tone, emotion, and nuance, adding a personal touch.

Visual Assets, like infographics and charts, simplify complex ideas into digestible formats. Tim Ferriss used visual summaries to convey key concepts, sharing them across social media to engage visually oriented audiences. These assets reinforce your message, expand your reach, and are particularly effective for those who prefer quick, visual information.

Incorporating multimedia content into your book promotion strategy ensures your message reaches a wide audience. This expanded reach enhances your book's impact and solidifies your position as a thought leader who caters to diverse audience needs.

From Content to Legacy

Building a legacy through a book involves leveraging that content to inspire, engage, and create a lasting impact. A book provides the foundation for thought leadership, but true influence comes from amplifying your message, refining your narrative, and aligning it with the needs of your audience over time.

Tim Ferriss demonstrated the power of strategic amplification with The 4-Hour Workweek. Through podcasts, PR campaigns, and multimedia platforms, he extended the reach of his book far beyond its initial release. His approach illustrates how consistent engagement and iterative storytelling can transform a single piece of content into a framework for lasting influence.

Liam Martin's journey with Running Remote shows how a book can serve as a launchpad for deeper engagement. By expanding on his ideas through conferences and podcasts, Liam built a community around the principles of remote work. His efforts highlight the value of creating a cohesive ecosystem where content, events, and discussions reinforce and expand the narrative.

Cherry Rose Tan leveraged her network and PR expertise to maximize the impact of her book, Still Standing. Her strategic planning ensured media coverage, created anticipation, and engaged her audience well before the book's release. This approach demonstrates the importance of early preparation and authentic connection in ensuring a successful launch.

These examples underline the critical role of strategic amplification in turning content into legacy. Adapting your message across multiple platforms allows you to reach diverse audiences while maintaining a unified narrative. Post-launch engagement, through activities like webinars, social media interactions, and live events, keeps your message alive and deepens its resonance with your audience.

A book is not just a standalone achievement—it's a catalyst for a long-term strategy that builds influence, fosters community, and shapes the conversation in your field. The process of iteration, engagement, and strategic amplification ensures your ideas remain relevant and transformative. In the next chapter, we'll delve into the entire Future Narrator Framework, providing a step-by-step guide to creating a framework that not only establishes authority but also leaves a lasting legacy.

Turning Content Into a Book
Download the Chapter Worksheet

Start transforming your content into a book with this structured worksheet.

resources.futurenarrator.com/book

CHAPTER 6

Bringing the Future Narrator Process to Life

Setting the Future Narrator Process in Motion

What does it take to turn bold ideas into a movement that shapes industries and inspires communities? Our Future Narrator Framework has been a systematic approach to transforming our raw vision into enduring impact. In this chapter, I want to share how we brought this framework to life, illustrating the transformative power of my 100X methodology and the collaborative synergy that drove the creation of this book. As we conclude Part 1 of this book, we wanted to combine the entire framework by demonstrating it, start to finish, to produce this book using Collision Conference 2024 in Toronto as our medium for conversations, community and thought leadership refinement.

Becoming a Future Narrator requires implementing ideas through a straightforward, actionable process that, when applied consistently, turns vision into legacy. I'll walk you through the entire process in three distinct 100-day sprints. The first sprint focused on establishing the Future Narrative, where we laid the foundation for our point of view (POV), vision and purpose. The second sprint emphasized amplifying the message, using tools like podcasting and social media to extend the reach of the interviews we conducted with 21 thought leaders at Collision Conference. Finally, the third sprint was dedicated to building a legacy, creating durable assets like our Podcast miniseries and this book to ensure the narratives endure and inspire for years.

My 100X methodology is the culmination of years of thoughts and journal entries about my observations on refining workflows to turn creative endeavours into transformative outcomes. When paired with Paul's expertise in content organization and book writing, it is a disciplined approach to content creation and execution that ensures progress on legacy assets while embracing iteration. The result is the Future Narrator Framework, the foundation for turning raw ideas into refined, impactful narratives that inspire communities.

Our Future Narrator year began with the hypothesis that great leaders inspire hope by sharing compelling, future-focused narratives. We believed that these narratives, when structured and refined, could align a leader's vision, philosophy, and business with the aspirations of their audience, creating movements and leaving lasting legacies. Throughout these sprints, we tested this hypothesis, refined our processes, and made tangible assets—including the podcast miniseries and this book. Our experience with this process demonstrated how we could scale the Future Narrator Framework for leaders seeking to align their vision with actionable outcomes and meaningful impact. Every step was an opportunity to learn, adapt, and grow, from podcasting to content creation and repurposing to the pre-release of this book. For me, the Future Narrator process reflects the power of structured thought leadership development—it proves that bold, consistent action can transform vision into a movement.

In the previous chapters, we showed how well-known and lesser-known leaders applied various elements of the Future Narrator Framework to develop their thought leadership. In this chapter, we'll walk you through the entire process in action to demonstrate its ability to guide founder CEOs in crafting, refining and evangelizing their Future Narrative. Let's dive into the sprints that made this vision a reality.

This sprint timeline outlines a strategic approach to building thought leadership and establishing yourself as the leading expert within a specific category.

Sprint 1

Days 1 - 100

Develop Point of View (POV)

Establish a compelling Future POV that defines a category and builds thought leadership.

Sprint 2

Days 101 - 200

Produce Podcast Series

Launch a podcast to refine and broadcast your message and grow an engaged community.

Sprint 3

Days 201 - 300

Publish Book

Transform the Future POV & podcast conversations into a published book as a legacy asset.

Future Narrator

This sprint model provides a structured roadmap for building thought leadership and creating a lasting impact within a chosen category.

Figure 2. Future Narrator Timeline

This timeline illustrates the three major sprints involved in transforming a Founder-CEO into a recognized Future Narrator:

1. Sprint 1–Days 1–100: Develop POV

Establish a forward-looking perspective (Future POV) that anchors your thought leadership and guides everything that follows.

2. Sprint 2–Days 101–200: Produce Podcast Series

Launch a podcast to refine your message, grow a community, and amplify your Future POV through conversations and shared insights.

3. Sprint 3–Days 201–300: Publish Book

Transform your most compelling ideas and podcast content into a published book, creating a lasting resource that cements your position as a leader in the field.

By visualizing these three sprints on a single timeline, the infographic gives you a clear roadmap—from developing your perspective, to scaling your voice, to building a legacy asset—that will be explored in greater detail throughout the rest of this chapter.

Sprint 1: Establishing the Future Narrative

How do you take something as abstract as a big idea in your head and turn it into a narrative that resonates with others and drives meaningful action? That was the question we aimed to explore during the first 100-day sprint. This phase was about understanding that turning a vision into a world-changing movement doesn't happen overnight. It simply begins with telling people your Point of View (POV) in a way that resonates and connects with them on a meaningful level.

The first 100-day sprint laid the foundation for what the Future Narrator Framework would become. This phase was both exciting and challenging. We were crafting a vision that would guide everything else. It started with asking big questions: What do leaders need to articulate their future vision? How can we build a system that helps them find and share their voice effectively?

Paul and I began by focusing on the core philosophy of the Future Narrator Framework. We knew that great leaders inspire hope by sharing compelling narratives about the future they're building. Beyond their products or services, these stories are about the bigger impact and change these leaders want to create. With this in mind, we built a framework to help leaders clarify and refine their vision into something actionable.

A key part of this sprint was testing our ideas in real time. You can make up all the hypotheses you like, but until you put them into action, you have no idea how they'll hold up. Working with the Future Narrator Framework during the Collision Conference project forced us to constantly test and refine it, ensuring our framework worked in theory and practice. Over three days, we conducted 21 podcast interviews with founder CEOs and industry leaders. Each interview was a chance to explore how these leaders were thinking about their future narratives. Were they clear on their vision? Were they able to articulate it in a way that inspired their audience? The answer was no for many, but that's where the real work began.

What struck me most during this sprint was how much potential these leaders had. Their passion and drive were evident even when their narratives were still unpolished. The interviews helped us identify the recurring challenge that leaders often struggled to distill their vision into a compelling message. They had big ideas but needed a structured process to bring those ideas into focus.

From these conversations, we created the Future Narrative POV document, a foundational tool in the Future Narrator Framework. This document became the blueprint for helping leaders articulate their vision. It's a starting point to capture what a leader stands for and where they want to go. Seeing this document take shape was a defining moment in this sprint. If you'd like to explore this tool further, the QR code to download the Future Narrative POV

Document is available at the end of Chapter 1. This showed that our process could take something abstract, a bold idea, and turn it into something tangible and actionable.

By the end of the sprint, we had tested and refined our hypotheses. We saw firsthand how important it is to meet leaders where they are and guide them step by step. This phase laid the groundwork for everything that came next. It proved that with the right tools and approach, any leader could craft a narrative that inspires and mobilizes others.

Sprint 2: Amplifying the Message

Once we had established the foundation during the first sprint, the next 100 days were all about amplification—taking the narratives we had started to build and ensuring they reached the right audiences. This phase felt like bringing the Future Narrator Framework to life. It's one thing to craft a compelling story and another to ensure it resonates with people and gains traction.

Sprint 2 focused on finding the best ways to share these narratives and experimenting with tools and platforms that could extend their reach. A big part involved transforming the podcast interviews we conducted during Collision Conference into a cohesive miniseries. We were repurposing the content and refining it for impact. Each episode was designed to showcase the leader's vision while also aligning with the broader themes of the Future Narrator Framework.

Sharing the podcast episodes on social media was a study in amplification. We observed the engagement and actively analyzed how people were responding. Which episodes sparked the most conversations? Which quotes resonated deeply enough to be shared? This feedback loop became an essential part of the sprint, helping us refine both our messaging and our approach.

What stood out most during this phase was the importance of interaction. Amplification isn't just about broadcasting a message—it's about starting a dialogue. By engaging directly with our audience, we could see what worked and what didn't. We wanted to understand how these narratives landed and where they needed adjustment. In this phase, we saw the actual value of collaboration as leaders and their teams began to share their perspectives on the process.

This discovery was a powerful moment of reflection. It reminded me of how much we often underrate ourselves and sell ourselves short. I realized that we had done so much great work, and an incredible amount of value was already within our reach. It's a matter of uncovering it. You won't find it until you start telling the story and amplifying your message. This feedback improved the book and reinforced the importance of amplifying your narrative to uncover the hidden gems within your journey. Imperfection is a necessary part of the creative process. By putting something imperfect out into the world, we gained the insights needed to improve it. You can't improve something you never created.

By the end of Sprint 2, we had amplified our narratives and deepened our understanding of how to connect with our audience. The key lesson of this phase is that amplification is more about resonance than volume. It's about ensuring that your message connects with them meaningfully. This sprint set the stage for what came next: building the legacy piece that would tie everything together.

Sprint 3: Building a Legacy

The final sprint involved bringing everything together to create a lasting impact. This legacy piece would stand as a product of the Future Narrator Framework and a resource for leaders looking to craft their own narratives. When you openly share your

Point of View (POV), interact with your community, and actively ask for feedback, the natural result is a distilled, potent, and engaging message. This approach draws people together around it, creating a shared sense of ownership and inclusion. For me, this phase demonstrated the full potential of our Future Narrator Framework through the lens of my 100X framework. How do you take everything you've learned, refined, and amplified and turn it into something enduring?

This sprint's primary focus was the book's writing and editing. By this point, we had a wealth of material to draw from—podcast interviews, feedback from the pre-release, and insights from social media interactions. The challenge was to distill all of that into a cohesive, compelling narrative that told our story and served as a guide for others. One thing that stood out during this phase was how iterative the process needed to be. Writing a book involves layering and refining content until it feels complete rather than writing a perfect draft.

One particularly novel aspect of this sprint was creating and printing the "C+ version"—a work-in-progress copy—and sharing it with trusted network members. One feedback that really stuck with me was a criticism of the examples we included. Some people felt the examples were all too big-name and out of reach. They wanted relatable, lesser-known examples. This prompted us to dive into my podcast archive, where we uncovered a wealth of stories from leaders I connected with—leaders who embody the principles of the Future Narrator Framework in authentic and approachable ways.

The "C+ version" feedback played a critical role in shaping the final product. It reminded us to focus on relatability, highlight examples that felt accessible, and share stories that resonated with the everyday challenges leaders face. This allowed us to create a narrative that was both personal and universal—grounded in real-world application but aspirational in its message.

Our community was involved at every step, from sharing drafts to gathering feedback. By opening up the book's development, we gained perspectives we could never have seen. Thought leadership becomes much more potent when it's a conversation than a monologue.

Another key focus was preparing for the book's launch. We wanted to ensure this wasn't just a one-time release but a cornerstone of a more significant movement. That meant thinking about positioning the book as a resource that would continue to inspire and educate. Whether through podcasts, speaking engagements, or social media campaigns, the goal was always to amplify the message and ensure it reached the people who needed it most.

By the end of Sprint 3, we had created something that encapsulated everything the Future Narrator Framework stands for. Our book is a living example of the framework in action. It's the result of bold ideas paired with disciplined execution. We created a proof of concept reinforcing the importance of action, iteration, and collaboration in building a legacy. It isn't about perfection but progress and the willingness to keep going.

The Future is Yours to Define

The Future Narrator Framework is a process that takes leaders on a structured yet flexible journey to refine their vision, amplify their message, and build enduring legacies. Throughout three 100-day sprints, we tested, iterated, and evolved this process, creating a system that transforms bold ideas into tangible movements.

The first sprint focused on establishing the Future Narrative, helping leaders clarify their vision and articulate a compelling Point of View. The second sprint emphasized amplifying the message, using tools like podcasts, social media, and feedback loops to expand the reach of their narratives. Finally, the third sprint was about building a legacy and creating durable assets like this book to inspire and educate future leaders.

One of the most valuable lessons we learned throughout this process is the power of community. By sharing our work openly, inviting feedback, and engaging in dialogue, we were able to create something far greater than what we could have done in isolation. Thought leadership isn't about broadcasting—it's about collaboration. Leaders who include others in their journey strengthen their message and build a movement around their vision.

Thank you for joining us on this journey through the Future Narrator Framework. Now, we invite you to embark on your own journey—to turn your bold ideas into enduring thought leadership that builds community and starts a movement. The world needs your vision more than ever, and it's time for you to make an impact.

Please revisit these six chapters and download the worksheets to build the components of your Future Narrative. You can also download the entire process here by scanning this QR code. We encourage you to contact us with your thoughts and comments—we'd love to acknowledge your insights in a future version of this book.

Implementing & Scaling Your Future Narrative
Download the Chapter Worksheet

Use this worksheet to apply and scale your thought leadership strategy.

resources.futurenarrator.com/scale

PIONEERING THE FUTURE: YOUR NEXT STEPS

You've reached the turning point. The Future Narrator framework is not just a philosophy—it's a movement. One that empowers you, as a leader, to shape the world through bold declarations, thought leadership, and meaningful action.

Now, it's time to take your next step.

Your Call to Action: Step Into Your Future Narrative

We designed our book's insights, strategies, and frameworks to help you refine your thought leadership and establish yourself as a category-defining leader. But knowledge alone isn't enough—execution is what separates visionaries from bystanders.

Here's how you can begin implementing everything you've learned:

1. Access the Full Future Narrator Resource Hub

We've developed a comprehensive resource hub where you can:

- Download the Full Future Narrator Workbook - Get all worksheets in one place.

- Develop and Define Your Point of View (POV) - Clarify your unique industry stance and craft your bold declaration.

- Explore the Future Narrator Framework - Follow the structured system to define, amplify, and scale your thought leadership.

- Join the Future Narrator Community via Substack - Connect with like-minded leaders, engage in discussions, and receive exclusive insights.

- Subscribe to the Future Narrator Substack - Stay updated with the latest thought leadership strategies.

- Book a Discovery Call with Flashpoint Global - Explore how we can help you scale your thought leadership.

- Learn More About Flashpoint Global - Understand how we empower founders to own and lead new categories through strategic narrative development and thought leadership.

Implementing & Scaling Your Future Narrative
Scan the QR Code below or visit
resources.futurenarrator.com/hub

Flashpoint Global: Transforming Founders into Category Leaders

At **Flashpoint Global**, we help founders and leaders become category-defining pioneers. Our mission is simple:

- **Inspire, Lead, Transform**
  - » Founders become catalysts for positive change, shaping their industries through visionary leadership.

- **Category Ownership**
  - » We don't just create brands—we craft movements that redefine industries and inspire transformation.

- **Simple Conversations, Powerful Outcomes**
  - » Through ongoing strategic discussions, we uncover and refine your unique perspective, transforming it into high-impact legacy content such as books, podcasts, and thought leadership initiatives.

2. Declare Your Future Narrative

A movement starts with a single statement. Make yours public. Post your Future Narrative Declaration on social media, your website, or even within your team. Need inspiration? Share it with us—we'll amplify it within the Future Narrator community.

- Use the hashtag #FutureNarrator and tag us to join the movement.

This is your Flashpoint—your moment to define the future. The only question is: Will you step into it?

Let's build the future together.

Edwin & Paul
Co-Creators, Future Narrator Movement

PART 2

Visionary leadership and innovative thinking can bring profound change across industries and communities. Leaders with great stories can build movements that shape the future. The following leaders were interviewed at Collision Conference as part of our podcast miniseries, and their stories have now been transformed into this book. By sharing their Future Visions, they leveraged their unique voices to redefine the boundaries of their fields.

The leaders introduced in this section are categorized into eight distinct areas of transformation:

1. Revolutionizing Financial Access and Empowering
2. Communities
3. Advancing Sustainable and Equitable Technology
4. Reimagining Customer Experiences in Retail
5. Optimizing Business Operations with Automation
6. Innovating Media and Content for Global Audiences
7. Transforming Healthcare with AI and Accessibility
8. Securing the Digital World with Cyber Resilience
9. Driving Industrial Transformation with Robotics

Whether they are reimagining customer experiences, empowering industries with automation, or securing the digital landscape, their stories usher people into the world they are innovating.

1. REVOLUTIONIZING FINANCIAL ACCESS AND EMPOWERMENT

These Future Narrators are addressing systemic barriers in finance, democratizing access and empowering individuals across income levels. By leveraging technology, they make financial services more inclusive, transparent, and tailored to underserved populations, reshaping finance for accessibility and security.

Liza Landsman
Democratizing Wealth for All
https://www.stash.com/

Liza Landsman is CEO of Stash, the pioneering fintech company that empowers everyday Americans to invest and build better lives. Landsman has spent her career scaling products and services that help people save and spend wisely, and is deeply committed to companies that address income inequality. Prior to Stash, Landsman served as General Partner at NEA, where she focused across consumer, e-commerce, wellness, and fintech sectors. Previously to that, Landsman was President of Jet. com and a founding member of the executive team from launch to its acquisition by Wal-Mart; following Jet's acquisition, she joined Wal-Mart's U.S. e-commerce

leadership team. She also served as Chief Marketing Officer and a member of the Executive Committee at E*TRADE Financial, Global Head of Digital for BlackRock, and held various leadership roles at both Citigroup and IBM earlier in her career. Landsman is an independent Board Director for Choice Hotels (CHH), Squarespace, and Applause App Quality and accolades include Forbes 50 Over 50, Fortune's Most Powerful Women One to Watch, and the NOW Women of Power and Influence network. She lives in New York City.

A Shift in the Wealth Management Industry

"Wealth management in the United States is a fantastic industry if you happen to be one of the 12.5 percent of U.S. households who are mass affluent," says Liza Landsman, CEO of Stash. For everyone else—the 87.5 percent of households— the financial system has remained inaccessible, full of barriers that make investing and wealth building a daunting task. The industry is experiencing a shift. With the rise of technology and platforms like Stash, the once impenetrable world of wealth management is opening up.

Previously excluded people are becoming financially literate and beginning to build assets, while traditional banks that failed to adapt are being left behind. Stash is stepping into this gap, making financial services approachable and accessible to low and middle-income individuals by allowing people to invest with as little as one or five dollars. "Our average customer invests $30 at a time," Landsman notes, emphasizing how small steps can lead to meaningful financial progress.

Ushering Customers into the New Financial World

In the old financial world, wealth building required substantial capital, specialized knowledge, and often a personal financial advisor. Today, Stash has made investing accessible to everyone, regardless of income. The company uses AI to provide personalized guidance and educational tools that help users make informed financial decisions. As Landsman puts it, "AI allows both providers and consumers of wealth management services to sort through and find more signal and less noise."

A single mother, for instance, who once believed she couldn't afford to invest due to the high costs and entry barriers of traditional financial services can now steadily build her financial foundation by investing 30 dollars at a time. Guided by Stash's AI money coach, she can also gain confidence along the way. Stash helps customers transition smoothly from the old financial world to the new by simplifying the process and providing the tools to overcome fear.

The Vision of an Empowered Financial Future

Imagine a future where financial security is accessible because everyone has the tools and knowledge to manage their finances effectively. "Our vision is that every low and middle-income consumer in America has Stash in their pocket," says Landsman. Financial literacy and asset-building are widespread, and growth opportunities are available to everyone, regardless of income or background. With Stash, financial stress and insecurity become things of the past, and individuals from all walks of life can pursue their dreams.

Stash's Financial Empowerment Tools

Stash equips its users with a range of powerful tools, giving them the ability to take control of their financial destinies:

- **AI-Powered Learning Modules:** These modules enhance financial literacy by simplifying complex concepts.

- **Low-Cost Investment Options:** With accessible, low-cost options, anyone can start investing.

- **AI Money Coach:** This personalized advisor provides tailored guidance while removing the embarrassment of telling someone you don't understand.

- **Auto-Stash Feature:** By automatically deducting small amounts for investment, users' wealth grows steadily without constant attention.

- **Gamified Savings Features:** Stash transforms the often-daunting task of saving into something fun by making saving engaging and interactive.

Landsman shares, "Financial empowerment and financial security come from having a sense of confidence and control over your finances." Stash is bridging the wealth management gap by making financial tools and education accessible to all. By addressing both the practical and psychological barriers to investing, Stash is transforming how low and middle-income Americans engage with their finances, making the dream of financial security a reality for everyone.

Eva Wong

Empowering Financial Confidence for Everyone

https://borrowell.com/

Eva is Co-Founder and Chief Operating Officer at Borrowell, a fintech that helps people feel confident about money. Borrowell offers free credit scores and reports as well as personalized financial product recommendations. Borrowell also helps people build credit with Credit Builder and Rent Advantage, Canada's first tenant-driven rent reporting product. With over 3 million members and 1 million mobile app users, Borrowell is one of largest consumer fintech companies in Canada. Eva and her co-founder Andrew Graham are EY Entrepreneur Of The Year® winners in Ontario. Eva enjoys baking, travelling and puzzles.

Personal Finance is a Maze Without a Map

For too many people, navigating personal finance feels overwhelming. There's an asymmetry of information—banks and lenders hold all the cards while consumers are left in the dark, often resulting in confusion, stress, and even shame. As co-founder and COO of Borrowell, Eva Wong, points out, "In a lot of families, it's a taboo subject... and that makes the problem worse." With 3 million members, Borrowell knows firsthand that people aren't just unsure how to improve their financial situation—many don't even know where to start. Access to essential financial tools, knowledge, and opportunities has traditionally been out of reach, particularly for those who need it most.

Putting Control Back in Consumers' Hands

Borrowell is tackling this problem by making personal finance more transparent and accessible. The company helps people understand and build their credit with easy-to-use tools, enabling them to make informed decisions. Borrowell offers free credit scores, education, and innovative services like Rent Advantage, which allows renters to report their rent payments to credit bureaus, levelling the playing field with homeowners.

Borrowell's platform provides a holistic approach to personal finance. Users can monitor their credit scores, receive personalized financial product recommendations, and access tools like Credit Builder to improve their creditworthiness over time. The Rent Advantage service connects directly with a tenant's bank account for automatic verification or rent payments, which are then submitted to credit bureaus to build their credit history. Borrowell also offers proactive insights and personalized suggestions, such as refinancing options or ways to reduce interest payments, enabling users to take practical steps toward financial improvement.

As Eva explains, "We want to live in a world where people feel confident about money," Borrowell is dedicated to providing "the insights and tools to help people make smart money decisions." By empowering people to monitor their credit and providing tailored recommendations, Borrowell is simplifying personal finance and giving people the power to take charge of their financial futures.

A World Where Financial Stress is a Thing of the Past

Eva Wong envisions a future where financial stress is minimized and people feel empowered and confident in managing their money. She imagines a proactive system that works for people. "Our vision is for people to feel confident about money because we're providing the insights and tools to help them make smart money decisions," says Eva. In this future, Borrowell will help consumers stay on top of their finances and anticipate their needs, from mortgage renewals to insurance updates, ultimately allowing individuals to focus less on financial worries and more on living their best lives.

Andrew Curtis

Fast, Flexible Funding That Lets Founders Stay in Control

https://clear.co/

Andrew Curtis is the CEO of Clearco. Andrew has over twenty years of experience working in finance in New York City, including roles at investment banks Merrill Lynch & Co. and Lazard Frères as well as several investment managers. Before joining Clearco as an advisor in July 2022, he served as an advisor to Annaly Capital Management, a real estate investment trust focused on housing finance and the residential mortgage market.

Andrew has an extensive background in leveraged credit, liability management and financial restructurings, asset-based finance and securitizations. He graduated from Brown University and subsequently earned master's degrees from the University of Chicago Graduate School of Business and The Fletcher School of Law & Diplomacy at Tufts University.

Traditional Funding Models Force Founders to Sacrifice

Imagine building a successful e-commerce business, only to find that the capital you need to grow could cost you ownership of your company or put your personal assets at risk. Before Clearco, many founders faced a harsh choice: equity financing, which meant giving up significant control over their startups, or traditional bank loans that required personal guarantees and collateral. The funding process was slow and cumbersome, often leaving entrepreneurs without the capital they needed at critical moments, forcing them to compromise their vision or risk everything. This environment stifled innovation and growth, making it difficult for promising startups to reach their full potential.

Clearco Offers Fast, Non-Dilutive Capital for Growth

Under Andrew Curtis's leadership, Clearco is revolutionizing how e-commerce entrepreneurs secure the capital they need to grow. "Clearco was created to fund working capital for e-commerce businesses in a non-dilutive way," Curtis explains. By offering a revenue-based financing model, Clearco empowers founders to access essential funds without sacrificing equity or ownership. This approach addresses one of the biggest challenges for entrepreneurs—finding capital without giving up control—allowing them to focus on scaling their businesses while retaining full authority over their vision.

"We provide revenue-based financing without requiring collateral or a personal guarantee," Curtis says. This model removes the traditional barriers of financing, making it a safer and more attractive option for founders. Additionally, Clearco's funding process is designed for speed and flexibility. "Many of our customers need capital fast. They want to raise it and deploy it quickly," Curtis notes. By delivering quick, adaptable funding, Clearco enables e-commerce businesses to seize opportunities as they arise, fueling growth without the usual delays and constraints.

Clearco uses AI and machine learning to improve the precision and efficiency of its funding process. "AI and machine learning have always been a core part of our business," Curtis says. By using these advanced technologies to assess creditworthiness and manage risk, Clearco ensures that funding decisions are accurate and swift, enabling them to provide tailored financial solutions for each e-commerce business.

After expanding rapidly into multiple products and global markets, Clearco has strategically refocused on its core mission—concentrating on its primary product, invoice funding, within the U.S. "The product is invoice funding, and the focus is the United States," Curtis says. This shift aligns with the current market's emphasis on discipline and efficiency, ensuring Clearco stays true to its mission: empowering entrepreneurs with the capital they need to succeed while maintaining a sustainable, scalable business.

A Scalable Future for Founder-Led Growth

"In an ideal world, we're expanding our products and entering adjacent markets," Curtis says, highlighting a vision for long-term diversification and growth. Throughout this journey, Clearco remains committed to transparency and open communication within the organization, fostering employee trust and morale. Most importantly, Clearco stays dedicated to its North Star—empowering entrepreneurs with the capital they need to succeed. This founding commitment drives every business decision and strategic direction, ensuring Clearco remains a reliable partner for entrepreneurs on their path to success.

2. SUSTAINABLE AND EQUITABLE TECHNOLOGY IN A CHANGING WORLD

Leaders in this category focus on aligning technology with environmental sustainability and social equity. By addressing climate change, accessibility, and responsible technology use, they ensure technological progress benefits society and the planet.

Winston Morton

Can We Turn Every Home into a Climate Solution?

https://www.climative.ai

Mr. Winston Morton is a Co-Founder and serves as Chief Executive Officer and Board Member at Climative. He served as Chief Technology Officer and Advisor at Climative. He is a dynamic, entrepreneurial professional who is adept at driving the growth of company revenue through the use of technology. His career has been focused on building new businesses, securing customer loyalty, and forging strong relationships with external business partners. He is an engaged mentor, active investor, and start-up community supporter. He gives back to his community through his volunteer work including as a Board member of Halifax Partnership. He has an Electrical Engineering Degree.

"Imagine a future where your home not only saves you money but also helps reverse climate change—without any extra effort." This is the vision that Winston Morton, CEO of Climative, aims to bring to life. Homeowners can upgrade their homes to be energy-efficient, reduce carbon emissions, and save money, all without disrupting their daily routines. By leveraging advanced AI technologies and collaborating with communities, governments, and financial institutions, Climative makes sustainable living simple and seamless.

Winston believes that sustainability should seamlessly integrate into everyday life. With Climative's leadership, sustainable living is no longer optional; it is essential. Homeowners can help create a greener planet while experiencing increased comfort and financial savings.

The Urgent Need for Change

Buildings contribute nearly 20% of global carbon emissions, but only 1-2% of homes are retrofitted each year—far short of the 4% needed to meet crucial climate targets. This gap represents a significant challenge for climate action. Winston Morton understands this issue and, through AI, is making energy efficiency upgrades more accessible and affordable. Climative is working to close this gap. "We must improve by 300-400% to hit our climate targets," says Winston, positioning Climative as a leader in this transformation.

Upgrading your home is more than just saving money—it's a way to contribute to a cleaner, healthier future. Climative empowers homeowners to take control and make energy-efficient living achievable. With Climative, sustainability feels like progress, not a sacrifice. Imagine the comfort of a home always at the right temperature, with lower energy bills and fewer worries. These upgrades not only enhance comfort but also protect the planet.

Every retrofit adds value to your home, and Climative ensures these improvements pay for themselves. "Every single building has a positive return on investment," Winston says, emphasizing both short-term savings and long-term benefits for homeowners.

Simplifying Energy Efficiency for Homeowners

The retrofitting process can be overwhelming, involving complex assessments, contractor coordination, and regulatory challenges. Despite the high cost of energy assessments, only 50% lead to completed projects. Climative simplifies this process with its AI-driven platform, which creates low-carbon plans tailored to each home and provides clear, actionable steps. Homeowners receive instant, data-driven recommendations, making energy upgrades easy and effective. Winston says, "Our platform uses artificial intelligence to pre-assess entire cities or provinces." Climative can scale solutions efficiently and offer recommendations faster than traditional methods. By starting the conversation with homeowners early and providing instant insights, Climative empowers them to make informed, environmentally responsible decisions.

To meet climate targets, Climative is leading the effort by using AI and partnering with municipalities, utilities, and financial institutions. "We work with cities, utilities, and provinces to lead the conversation," Winston notes. New regulations incentivize banks to support green initiatives, making financing more accessible for homeowners. By making retrofits affordable and accessible, Climative enables homeowners to contribute to a greener future without the typical cost and complexity barriers.

Equitable access to energy efficiency is critical. "The federal government is shifting programs to offer more upfront incentives, even covering 100% of retrofit costs for some," Winston explains. This ensures that low-income households can access the benefits of energy-efficient homes, including lower bills and improved comfort. Climative works alongside government programs to ensure that everyone can participate in the energy transition regardless of income. This inclusive approach is crucial for a sustainable, equitable future.

Winston Morton envisions a future where homes generate more energy than they consume. Imagine waking up in a solar-powered home, with excess energy feeding back into the grid to support neighbors. You're not just conserving energy; you're contributing to a cleaner, more sustainable future. By the end of the month, your utility bills could even be positive—earning you money for the energy your home provides. The future is here—are you ready to join the movement?

Emma Todd

Leading Blockchain to a Greener, More Inclusive Future

https://mmhgroup.io/

Emma is CEO of MMH Technology Group, & is Chair of the Canadian Blockchain Consortium's Mining Committee, a board member of the Canadian Blockchain Consortium and Chair for Girls In Tech.

Disrupting Finance in a Traditional World

Emma Todd, CEO of MMH Technology Group, has been at the forefront of blockchain technology since 2016, carving a path in a sector that is both exciting and rife with challenges. "We are trying to disrupt how financial services work," she shares. This disruption aims to democratize access to financial systems and make them more transparent and accessible. However, Emma quickly learned that the incumbents in finance and government would not sit back and let this revolution happen quietly. "The banks are fighting back, big time. The governments, too," she admits, reflecting on her journey and the early naivety about the difficulties of disrupting deeply entrenched systems.

When Emma entered the blockchain space, she was surrounded by brilliant engineers who were passionate about building but needed direction on bringing their products to market. "They were like, 'If we build it, they will come.' And I had to tell them, 'No, you need marketing, you need a strategy,'" she recalls. This realization led Emma to create MMH Technology Group, a consulting firm focused on helping blockchain companies build great products, market them effectively, and navigate complex regulatory landscapes.

Building Trust and Environmental Responsibility

Emma's work isn't just about consulting but also hands-on innovation. She moved into Bitcoin mining, helping miners find environmentally friendly ways to power their operations. "We realized what we were doing wasn't necessarily as good for the environment as everyone thought," she says. Emma didn't shy away from the criticism but instead found solutions. One such solution was utilizing methane gas—traditionally an environmental hazard—to generate electricity for Bitcoin mining. "We found a way to siphon off methane gas and use it to make electricity to mine Bitcoin. Nobody else in any other industry is really doing that," she notes with pride.

Emma also highlights the need for constant adaptation in this volatile space. "You can't stand still. You have to be like a palm tree during a hurricane—you bend, but you don't break," she says. With only 1.5 million Bitcoins left to mine, Emma is already looking ahead, positioning her company for a future in AI data centers. "We have a really good plan that's working out," she says, emphasizing the importance of planning not just for today but for the next three to five years.

A Billion-Dollar Company that Changes Perceptions

Emma's vision is to change the narrative around blockchain, Bitcoin mining, and the role of women and minorities in tech. "We want better adoption for blockchain companies, a recognition that we're really doing good things and that we're not the enemy," she says. Her ambitions are big: "My vision is to build a billion-dollar company," she states, emphasizing her commitment to Environmental, Social, and Governance (ESG) standards. Emma wants to be a role model for women and minorities. "More women need to be recognized for being smart and doing great things. I don't see limits—I just see what I want to do, and I do it," she asserts.

Emma's journey is one of resilience, vision, and community. She is leading a movement that changes how people perceive blockchain and mining. "The community didn't care what I looked like; they just cared that I could help," she recalls, underscoring the inclusive spirit that keeps her motivated. With her eyes set firmly on the future, Emma Todd is determined to lead her company—and the blockchain industry—towards a more sustainable, equitable, and connected world.

Bob Beachler

The Next Leap in AI Requires Smarter, Greener Solutions

https://www.untether.AI/

Bob Beachler is a Silicon Valley veteran and proven senior executive with industry leaders such as Altera, Xilinx, and BrainChip. He brings to the company a wealth of experience in the development and marketing of FPGAs, software tools, vision processors and artificial intelligence acceleration devices.

As AI reshapes industries and redefines possibilities, it also brings with it a pressing challenge: managing the immense energy demands that could "end up burning down the planet," warns Bob Beachler, Chief Product Officer at Untether AI.

AI's Growth Is Unsustainable Without Efficiency

The surge in AI workloads drives massive power consumption, with traditional CPUs and GPUs struggling to keep up. Untether AI is stepping in to tackle this critical issue, offering groundbreaking solutions that drastically cut the energy required for AI operations, ensuring that the future of AI is both powerful and sustainable.

AI's rapid integration into technologies like smartphones and autonomous vehicles is driving an unprecedented demand for computational power. This surge is escalating operational costs and posing significant environmental challenges. Traditional processors, designed before the AI revolution, struggle to meet these demands efficiently.

Untether AI Delivers Scalable, Sustainable AI Solutions

Untether AI's innovative approach reimagines AI processing to significantly lower power consumption and minimize the carbon footprint.

The AI industry is also grappling with supply chain disruptions, and the challenge goes beyond current hardware demands. The next wave of AI deployment is focused on inference, which refers to using trained AI models to make real-time decisions or predictions for various applications. The demand for processing power will skyrocket. Millions of devices, from smartphones to autonomous vehicles, needing to perform AI inference could push the supply chain to breaking point. Untether AI addresses this dual problem with scalable, energy-efficient technologies that ease current supply chain pressures and prepare for widespread AI inference deployment, ensuring the industry can meet future demands sustainably.

As AI becomes increasingly embedded in everyday life, it will redefine how we interact with technology across platforms—from smart homes to healthcare and transportation. AI will automate complex tasks, driving efficiency and enhancing human productivity. By managing routine, labour-intensive work, AI will free time for creative and strategic pursuits. Achieving this vision sustainably requires energy-efficient solutions to ensure its widespread deployment supports productivity and the planet's health.

A Future Where AI Empowers Without Compromising the Planet

Bob Beachler envisions a future of deep personalization, with "millions of models all tailored for specific applications in specific regions," driving innovation across diverse markets. "Our vision is that we become the inference solution," Bob says, emphasizing the company's commitment to efficient and sustainable AI technologies. Untether AI is positioning itself to redefine how AI enhances productivity and integrates into every aspect of life. "I believe it's going to make us better. It's not going to replace jobs. It's just going to make you more productive," he asserts.

While he acknowledges that the development of Artificial General Intelligence (AGI) is still far off, he believes that AGI's eventual impact will further revolutionize how we interact with technology. "We're adaptable, and we can change AI," Bob says, emphasizing the ongoing innovation and adaptability that will lead to continuous improvements and new applications. By making AI more efficient and sustainable, Bob sees a world where AI, and eventually AGI, will drive long-term growth, create new opportunities, and help build better lives for everyone.

3. TRANSFORMING CUSTOMER EXPERIENCES IN RETAIL AND E-COMMERCE

These Future Narrators reimagine the retail journey, creating personalized, integrated, and elevated customer experiences. By unifying digital and physical interactions, they empower businesses of all sizes to meet modern consumer demands.

Marcus Rader

Thriving in the Complex World of Vacation Rentals

https://www.hostaway.com/

I started my first company when I was 11. Since then I've been learning about the world of business, growing up in an environment where global communication and connectivity gets better each day. With 10 years of experience in online marketing at various startups, it's time to help others.

The Transformative Shift in Vacation Rentals

The vacation rental industry is undergoing a major transformation, where simply listing a property on platforms like Airbnb is no longer enough to turn a profit. Property managers now face a fragmented landscape where different platforms handle various aspects inconsistently, such as guest ID verification, payment processing, and bookings. This inconsistency creates operational challenges, making it difficult for property managers to oversee their properties efficiently.

Marcus Rader describes this shift: "Originally, we spoke to a bunch of people, and they said, 'Here's the problem: I'm listed on Airbnb, but they don't fill my calendar.' Then came more problems: Airbnb does ID checks, but other platforms don't." Hostaway addresses these fragmented experiences by offering a unified platform that automates bookings, synchronizes calendars, and integrates maintenance scheduling. This comprehensive solution allows property managers to focus on what truly matters—providing exceptional guest experiences.

A Vision of Effortless Management

Hostaway's platform empowers property managers with the tools they need to deliver flawless guest experiences. Automated processes, synchronized calendars, and dynamic pricing optimize each booking and delight every guest. Managing a vacation rental business becomes feasible and profoundly rewarding, and property managers can concentrate on growth and relationships rather than getting bogged down by daily tasks.

Hostaway's Tools that Empower Property Managers

Hostaway's platform offers powerful features that help property managers navigate the complexities of the vacation rental industry.

These tools include:

- Automated Booking Management: AI-driven booking automation saves time and eliminates errors, allowing property managers to focus on growth.

- Unified Communication Hub: Property managers can ensure they never miss an important email or lose a booking by centralizing guest communication.

- Dynamic Pricing Algorithms: Hostaway's advanced pricing tools stay ahead of the market and maximize revenue.

- Guest Verification Tools and Maintenance Scheduling: Comprehensive guest checks and automated maintenance reminders help property managers be proactive and always in control.

Transformations with Hostaway

Marcus Rader highlights that local property managers who are well-connected in their communities are thriving: "The local ones, managing 10 or 20 properties, know every plumber and restaurant owner in their area. They are shining and thriving right now." By equipping these managers with essential tools, Hostaway helps them streamline operations, boost revenue, and enhance guest satisfaction. Hostaway's innovative solutions enable property managers to succeed in the competitive vacation rental market.

Alyson Zhang

Empowering Small Retailers to Compete in a Digital World

https://www.shoplazza.com/

An enthusiastic innovator with expertise in legal frameworks and AI technology, dedicated to revolutionizing retail through smart SaaS solutions. Shoplazza's product is missioned to seamlessly integrate online and offline shopping, transforming retail into an exciting journey of exploration. With a proven track record in founding and scaling startups, I focus on enhancing customer experiences and driving operational efficiency, making retail smarter and more intuitive.

Where Shopping Falls Short Today

Today's retail environment presents a fragmented and frustrating shopping journey for customers. Whether it's the disconnect between online and in-store experiences, lack of personalization, or inconsistent service across channels, the result is often dissatisfaction and missed engagement opportunities. Customers often find themselves moving between online and physical stores with inconsistent experiences. They want a seamless transition between these environments, but the reality is far from it. As Alyson points out, "Customers don't think in terms of channels—they just want a great experience, no matter where they are." The divide between in-store and online shopping results in frustration, and traditional retail models struggle to adapt to the digital demands of modern consumers.

Retailers, especially smaller businesses, struggle to keep up with evolving customer expectations and the technology needed to provide a cohesive experience. Limited resources leave them at a disadvantage compared to larger, tech-savvy competitors. Many smaller retailers lack the necessary tools to provide personalized and consistent service, leading to lost opportunities and an inability to meet customer needs effectively.

Making Shopping Personal, Immersive, and Seamless

Shoplazza is transforming the retail experience by using technology to make shopping more immersive and personalized. "Our goal is to use AI and data to understand each customer as an individual, to know what they want before they even ask for it," Alyson explains. Shoplazza gains deep insights into customer behaviours and preferences, allowing every interaction to be tailored to the individual shopper, creating an environment where customers feel understood and valued. Alyson is committed to making shopping exciting. "Shopping should be an experience, not a chore," she says.

Shoplazza's omni-channel approach integrates in-store and online shopping to create a unified experience. Whether a customer browses online, visits a store, or completes a purchase through an app, the experience remains consistent and fluid. By merging physical and digital shopping into one seamless experience, Shoplazza ensures that customers move effortlessly between environments, meeting the evolving expectations of today's consumers.

Empowering a Unified Retail Experience

Alyson Zhang envisions a seamless, personalized shopping experience that integrates online and offline channels. "The line between digital and physical retail is disappearing, and we need to be ready for that shift," she says. For Alyson's vision to succeed, it must be inclusive. Small and medium enterprises (SMEs) often struggle to compete with larger players with more resources and advanced technologies. "We want to empower smaller retailers to compete on the same level as the big brands," Alyson says. Through Shoplazza, she is breaking down these barriers by providing SMEs with accessible e-commerce solutions that help them deliver the same convenience, personalization, and efficiency as larger competitors.

Alyson's passion for enhancing the customer experience is evident in everything Shoplazza does—from intuitive interfaces to personalized recommendations. "Everything we do is about the customer. If we make their experience better, we win," she says. Shoplazza's platform adapts to each shopper's unique needs, transforming how people engage with brands and creating a unified marketplace where technology erases local and global commerce divisions. Alyson is building a thriving global community where everyone—from small business owners to consumers—has the opportunity to succeed and grow.

Robert Brunner

The Fusion of Technology and Humanity in Design

https://ammunitiongroup.com

Robert founded Ammunition in 2007 to communicate ideas through products, brands, and their surrounding experiences. His work as an industrial designer has spawned numerous brand- defining designs over the past three decades. Prior to founding Ammunition, Robert was a partner at Pentagram and led strategic brand consulting and industrial design programs for Fortune 500 companies. Previously, he was the Director of Industrial Design for Apple, where he established its pioneering internal corporate design organization, Apple IDge.

When Robert Brunner led Apple's design team in its early days, he helped lay the foundation for a revolution where technology became an extension of the human experience. Today, as the founder of Ammunition Group, he continues to push the boundaries of how products interact with people, blending technology with human-centred design. His guiding philosophy, "Technology enables, design establishes," drives his approach to innovation. Technology provides the tools to create, but design breathes life into a product, giving it purpose and meaning in people's lives.

In the past, design was a slow, manual process, with designers spending countless hours drafting and creating physical models by hand. While this method encouraged precision and craftsmanship, it lacked a direct connection to real-time user needs. Today, technology has transformed the process. AI, rapid prototyping, and real-time feedback allow designers to work much faster and more efficiently. However, as Brunner emphasizes, the true value of a product comes from its design. Technical innovation alone is not enough; the key is to ensure the product connects with people on a deeper level. "It's not just about getting the technology right," Brunner says, "it's about making sure the design resonates with the people who use it."

How Technology Powers Design's Impact

Brunner believes the human touch in design is essential, even in a technology-driven world. While technology allows for quick innovation, the personal element in design transforms a product. For instance, consider an AI-powered memory augmentation tool created by a founder who has experienced hearing loss. This tool allows users to capture and store information seamlessly. However, the design, influenced by the founder's experience of reconnecting to the world through a hearing aid establishes an emotional connection with users, turning the tool into something deeply meaningful. Storytelling is one of the designer's most poignant devices.

Brunner ensures technology remains a tool in service of the user experience. Whether through AI-driven predictive analytics or VR-based product visualization, technology opens new possibilities. However, design is what grounds these innovations in human connection, turning products into experiences that resonate. As Brunner notes, "We're not just making things—we're creating relationships between people and products."

Balancing Speed and Emotion in Modern Design

As designers embrace AI and rapid prototyping, the temptation to focus solely on speed and efficiency is strong. However, Brunner insists that real success comes when design takes center stage. A product's emotional impact is what sets it apart from the competition. While technology offers the tools to make products faster and more intelligent, the emotional connection that design fosters makes them memorable. Products that speak to users personally stand out in the marketplace and become a lasting part of their lives.

Brunner's vision for the future of design emphasizes adaptability and sustainability. While technology enables rapid iteration, design ensures products remain relevant and meaningful over time. His focus on human-centred design guarantees that products are functional and emotionally resonant, allowing them to evolve alongside their users. Technology enables possibilities, but design gives those possibilities purpose, fostering deeper connections between people and the products they use.

Design as the Driver of Innovation

In a world where technology is advancing rapidly, Brunner clearly states that technology provides the tools for progress, but design defines how that progress will improve the human experience. As products become more integrated into our lives, design will continue to play the crucial role of ensuring those products enhance our interactions with the world and each other.

The future of design isn't just about keeping up with technological advancements—it's about creating products that enrich human experiences. As Robert Brunner continues to champion the fusion of technology and human-centred design, his message is clear: the future belongs to those who dare to imagine new ways of connecting people and products. Now is the time for innovators, entrepreneurs, and designers to rethink how technology can serve a higher purpose. By putting design at the heart of innovation, we can shape a future where products function and form lasting, meaningful relationships with their users.

4. BUILDING CONNECTED, AUTOMATED, AND SCALABLE BUSINESS SOLUTIONS

This category focuses on optimizing business operations through AI, automation, and data analytics. These leaders streamline complex tasks and enhance efficiency, competitiveness, and customer-centricity in diverse business environments.

Jason Smith

Competitive Intelligence in the Age of AI

https://klue.com/

Product driven, sales and marketing centric tech entrepreneur. Cofounder, investor or early employee of 5 start-ups. Former President, Vision Critical (startup to 500+ people), VP of Electronic Arts and Cofounder of web applications pioneer Columbus Group (acquired by TELUS, NYSE: TU). I've led sales, marketing, product and services teams, advised great companies like Mobify (mobile commerce engagement acquired by Salesforce.com) and Strutta (social engagement platform acquired by LX Ventures) and received E&Y's Emerging Entrepreneur of the Year for the Pacific Region. Now baking Klue to give companies a lens into their competitors world.

The world of B2B sales is changing faster than ever before. With the rise of advanced AI technologies and the shifting economic landscape, the rules of the game are being rewritten. Companies face tighter budgets and the challenge of managing increasing competition in their industries. Jason Smith, CEO of Klue, sees winners and losers in this dynamic environment. "Tech is the first to spend and the first to pull back," says Jason, highlighting the challenges faced by many B2B companies. Those who struggle are often blind to the competitive landscape, losing out on opportunities they should have won because they simply lack the right intelligence. But those who thrive can quickly adapt, leveraging insights to outmaneuver competitors and win deals.

Moving from Guesswork to Strategic Action

Klue transforms how businesses approach competitive intelligence and win-loss analysis, ushering their customers into a world where insights, not guesswork, guide decision-making. In the old world, sales teams often relied on incomplete or outdated information— "I remember being on a call, and the prospect knew more about our competitor than we did," Jason recalls. This is the old world: fragmented information, lost opportunities, and a lack of clarity.

With Klue, the new world looks vastly different. Using Klue's platform, companies gain real-time insights into their competitors' activities—be it a product launch, a pricing change, or shifts in marketing strategy. They can see where they stand relative to competitors and act strategically. For example, Klue's win-loss analysis enables companies to understand why they are losing deals, providing direct buyer feedback that often reveals misalignment in messaging, product fit, or customer engagement. As Jason puts it, "It's not just about data; it's about turning that data into action and empowering teams to adapt in real-time."

A Future Where Knowledge Closes the Competitive Revenue Gap

"Every company in the world has three things in common: employees, customers, and competitors," says Jason. Klue's vision is to be the "system of record" for competitive intelligence, helping every business understand its position and outmaneuver its competitors. In this future, companies will be proactive, not reactive; they will understand their market and their competition as deeply as they understand their offerings. Sales teams are empowered, marketing strategies are sharpened, and every department—from product management to talent acquisition—is aligned with a clear understanding of where they stand relative to the competition.

Empowering Companies with Competitive Superpowers

Klue equips companies with unique tools that fundamentally change how they engage with competition. The platform provides an "always-on" stream of intelligence, constantly monitoring competitors' moves—whether that's tracking changes on their websites, shifts in messaging, or even the awards they're winning. This allows sales teams to "elegantly maneuver" during conversations, confidently addressing prospects' concerns with up-to-date information rather than relying on outdated wikis or potentially incorrect assumptions. Klue also empowers companies through buyer interviews, providing unfiltered insights directly from the prospects they won or lost. "Sixty-three percent of data in the CRM is wrong," says Jason. With Klue, companies replace those incorrect assumptions with hard truths—revealing, for example, that a lost deal wasn't about pricing but about cultural fit or messaging that missed the mark.

Turning Insights into Action

Many companies have already made the leap from the old world of guesswork to the new world of intelligence-driven action with Klue. Nike, for example, used Klue's competitive intelligence platform to refine their talent acquisition strategy. They compared their company culture with that of competitors and leveraged those insights to attract top talent that was the right fit for their organization. By understanding how they stacked up against competitors in the eyes of potential employees, Nike made strategic adjustments that ultimately strengthened their employer brand and improved hiring outcomes.

The line between success and failure is no longer determined by guesswork but by the ability to transform intelligence into action. As Klue continues to empower organizations to thrive, the winners of tomorrow will be those who embrace knowledge, adaptability, and proactive strategies to outpace their competition and capture the opportunities they deserve.

Derric Gilling

Unlock API Potential and Turn Data into Revenue

https://www.moesif.com

Derric Gilling is the CEO of Moesif, the leading API analytics and monetization platform. He enjoys working with both startups and large enterprises on launching and scaling an API-first strategy. Gilling is a frequent speaker at developer conferences, including API World, Developer Week, APIDays, and DevRelCon. Gilling has also authored various reports on APIs, including O'Reilly and Nordic APIs.

Are Your APIs Leaving Money on the Table?

In today's digital age, APIs (Application Programming Interfaces) are the invisible connectors. They are the bridges that link cloud services, mobile apps, and different software tools, allowing companies to innovate and build experiences at an unprecedented pace. APIs facilitate digital transformation, empowering businesses to be more agile and responsive to customer needs. However, as companies increasingly rely on APIs, new challenges emerge. These include understanding how APIs are used, ensuring their reliability, and unlocking their full potential.

Revolutionizing API Management to Build Value

Moesif was founded to provide businesses with the observability and analytics tools to overcome these challenges.

"APIs are essential to the success of digital-first businesses, but without the right visibility, it becomes difficult to understand how your APIs are being used or where there may be issues," says Derric Gilling, CEO of Moesif. "We started Moesif because we wanted to make it easy for API providers to deeply understand how their APIs are being consumed and how to create value for their users," Gilling explains. Moesif helps companies optimize their APIs for reliability, performance, and user experience by offering actionable insights. Their platform provides end-to-end observability, allowing companies to gain a complete view of their API usage.

With Moesif, businesses can monitor key metrics like latency, error rates, and user engagement. For example, a company like NexHealth used Moesif to launch an API that allowed their customers to automate scheduling and other processes, enhancing efficiency and creating new value opportunities. "With Moesif, it's about more than just tracking API calls—it's about understanding the bigger picture," Gilling emphasizes. By providing these insights, Moesif enables product teams to proactively address issues and deliver a seamless experience for end users.

Moesif is not just a tool for developers—it is designed to be accessible to everyone involved in creating digital experiences, including designers, marketers, and other stakeholders. "We're not just a tool for ops or developers," Gilling notes. "Moesif is designed to be accessible to anyone who interacts with APIs, from product managers to customer success teams." By understanding how APIs are used, product managers can identify features that drive engagement, while customer success teams can pinpoint and resolve user pain points more effectively. This comprehensive visibility helps businesses improve customer experiences, increase adoption, and drive growth.

Driving Revenue in a Connected Digital Future

Building on Moesif's success, Gilling says, "Our goal is to continue to innovate and make API observability even more impactful for our customers." He envisions Moesif as an essential component of the API ecosystem, enabling businesses to leverage data for new revenue opportunities. Moesif aims to help companies become more like Stripe or Twilio, where APIs are not just a technical component but a revenue-generating opportunity.

By helping businesses understand and optimize their APIs, Moesif is shaping a more connected and efficient digital future. "We believe that APIs are the future of how software is built and delivered, and we're excited to help our customers make the most of this opportunity," says Gilling. With a clear mission and a focus on empowering teams across the organization, Moesif sets the standard for building, managing, and monetizing APIs, whether helping companies adopt usage-based billing models or guiding product teams in creating better customer experiences.

Jarrett Quan-Hin

Empowering Founders to Manage Their Most Finite Resource

https://withmantle.com/

Jarrett Quan-Hin is the co-founder and Head of Product at Mantle. Based in Toronto, Jarrett has led product development in the games, retail, automotive, and financial industries at companies such as Pivotal and Autonomic

Disconnect and Complexity in Equity Management

Managing equity has become overwhelming for many founders, often riddled with inefficiencies and confusion. "There's been a growing disconnect on how companies think about and reason with their cap tables," says Jarrett Quan-Hin, co-founder of Mantle. Cap tables are often assembled from complex legal documents, board consents, and filings, creating error-prone, disjointed data. Founders, their CFOs, and lawyers spend time navigating these complexities rather than focusing on the growth of their businesses. This situation worsens when companies export data to spreadsheets, increasing the risk of mismatches and mistakes in managing one of their most valuable resources—equity.

AI-Powered, Transparent Cap Table Management

Mantle is reimagining equity management by providing a platform that empowers founders to understand, manage, and plan their equity more efficiently. "We're building out an AI-powered onboarding process in which we are looking at the raw documents, extracting the key information, and then presenting it in a way that founders can quickly understand," explains Jarrett. By leveraging AI, Mantle ensures that cap tables are accurate and transparent, allowing founders to have a real-time health check of their equity. Mantle's approach also synthesizes data to clearly present actionable insights, enabling founders to make informed decisions without exporting data to spreadsheets or risking stakeholder miscommunication. Beyond onboarding, Mantle empowers founders by providing tools and educational resources, turning equity from an intimidating element to an accessible and manageable resource.

Building an Ecosystem That Empowers Execution

Jarrett's vision is to create an ecosystem where founders are empowered to make bold, strategic decisions without being bogged down by the complexities of equity management. "The more we can empower founders to utilize and think about equity properly, the better the entire product ecosystem is going to wind up being," Jarrett shares. Mantle is dedicated to shifting the equity paradigm from something founders often misunderstand to a powerful tool for growth and retention. By offering transparency, clear data, and an AI-driven approach, Mantle aims to free founders to focus on innovation and scaling their businesses—knowing their equity management is in good hands. In this vision, companies are equipped to stay private longer, confidently navigate funding rounds, and align stakeholders on a clear path forward.

Scott Boston

Insurance Reimagined for Small Businesses

http://www.foxquilt.com

https://disruptmagazine.com/dream-big-and-work-hard-a-founders-story-with-mark-morissette/ (reference) Mark Morissette, CEO and co-founder of Foxquilt, is a seasoned entrepreneur and visionary in the InsurTech industry. With a rich background in financial services and insurance, Mark has dedicated his career to transforming the insurance landscape through technology and innovation. His leadership at Foxquilt has led to the creation of customized insurance solutions tailored for small businesses and independent professionals, challenging traditional industry norms and providing value-driven products. Mark's strategic vision for Foxquilt emphasizes customer-first approaches, proprietary technology, and cross-border solutions, aiming to revolutionize insurance for businesses across North

America. His commitment to innovation, combined with a focus on fostering a diverse and inclusive team culture, marks him as a pivotal figure in the evolving InsurTech sector.

Traditional Insurance Doesn't Work for Small Businesses

Small businesses have long faced barriers when trying to secure insurance. From navigating a complex broker system to dealing with opaque pricing and lengthy approval processes, getting insured has often been an overwhelming experience. As Scott Boston, CFO of Foxquilt, describes, "It used to be that they would have to go to a broker, maybe they could get a quote online, but they'd still have to talk to someone, maybe go into an office... there's very little transparency in that." The lack of flexibility, customizability, and real-time accessibility in traditional insurance has left many small businesses either uninsured or paying too much for inadequate coverage.

Empowering Small Businesses with Data-Driven, Tailored Insurance

Foxquilt is changing the game by using technology to bring transparency, speed, and personalization to small business insurance. The company has built a high-tech, low-touch online platform that allows small business owners to access tailored insurance whenever and wherever they need it. Unlike traditional brokers who often rate small businesses on their most risky activity, Foxquilt's proprietary platform uses a data-driven "multi ISO basis" approach. This means customers are explicitly rated based on the percentage of activities they do, resulting in more accurate pricing and better coverage.

Foxquilt leverages machine learning and in-house IP to continually improve its offerings. The platform collects data with every new application, learning from successful and declined policies to ask better questions and create more precise recommendations. Scott explains, "Our machine continues to learn and ask new, more specific, and better questions with every application that comes in." This allows Foxquilt to offer small businesses policies that fit their unique needs—giving them everything they need and nothing they don't.

Through its embedded insurance approach, Foxquilt also partners with enterprises and brokers. Large enterprises, such as home improvement retailers, can easily onboard contractors and ensure they are adequately covered. At the same time, brokers use Foxquilt's platform to secure the right insurance for their clients efficiently. By integrating directly with enterprise systems and wholesale networks, Foxquilt ensures that insurance becomes a seamless part of the process for contractors, helping them get covered so they can get to work quickly.

A Connected, Fair Insurance Ecosystem

Foxquilt's vision is to build a connected insurance ecosystem that eliminates friction and ensures fair access to insurance for all. By providing carriers with access to a previously untapped market of small businesses and by offering small businesses tailored insurance that fits their needs, Foxquilt aims to create a win-win-win situation for all stakeholders. "We're that middle layer that reduces friction in the whole system and allows data to create a better overall system," Scott says.

Foxquilt plans to expand its offering beyond North America and into professional services like accounting, legal, and healthcare. By using its data-driven platform to support a broader range of professionals, Foxquilt aims to make the concept of shared risk—

the core principle of insurance—more inclusive and accessible. Ultimately, Scott envisions a world where insurance is proactive, personalized, and easy to access, empowering small businesses to thrive without the burden of outdated insurance models.

5. REDEFINING MEDIA AND CONTENT CREATION FOR GLOBAL AUDIENCES

By innovating content creation, adaptation, and distribution, these leaders bridge cultural and linguistic gaps. Their work ensures content resonates globally, inspiring productive engagement and making media accessible to audiences worldwide.

Hafu Go
Turning Content Consumption Into Inspiration

https://hafugo.odoo.com/

Hafu Go is a pan-Asian content creator boasting over 5 million subscribers on YouTube & 2 billion views. Now creating some of the largest "edutainment" content on YouTube. Having cracked the code as a hybrid creator, regularly achieving millions of views. SUBSCRIBERS. 6,350,000 VIDEO VIEWS 1,839,962,012 VIDEO COUNT 322 COUNTRY United States (US) CATEGORY Education YOUTUBER SINCE2017

Social Media Leaves Us Feeling Empty

Too often, consuming content on social media leaves people feeling drained and unproductive. As Hafu Go, a viral content creator and YouTuber, points out, social media is filled with content that creates a feeling of "brain rot." It's easy for viewers to get sucked into endless scrolling, with little to show for it besides wasted time. "People feel like they're wasting time when they're consuming content," Hafu explains, and that's a huge problem for an industry that should be capable of so much more. People crave more meaningful, enriching experiences but often find themselves stuck in an endless loop of fleeting, superficial content.

Inspiring Action Through Edutainment

Hafu Go is reshaping how people experience social media by creating content that educates, inspires, and motivates audiences to act. His content focuses on learning from experts in niche hobbies, like Rubik's cubes, and bringing that enthusiasm to a broader audience. Instead of producing entertaining content, Hafu aims to make every video "anti-brain rot." He turns their consumption into a productive, feel-good experience by making viewers feel inspired and educated. With his channel growing at a rate of about a million subscribers per month, Hafu leverages platforms like YouTube, using short-form and long-form content to meet audiences where they are—whether they're looking for a quick burst of insight or something more in-depth. His approach embraces YouTube's push towards TV-based content, allowing families to watch together and learn in an engaging, positive environment.

Content That Uplifts, Educates, and Inspires

Hafu Go envisions a future where social media isn't just a distraction but a powerful tool for growth. "I want to make content that educates people, inspires them, and makes them feel better about themselves," Hafu says. He aims to influence an entire generation by creating content that adds value to people's lives—helping viewers discover new interests, learn skills, and feel more connected to the world around them. In Hafu's future, social media is a force for good—a platform that motivates rather than drains and uplifts instead of numbing. By making content that feels good to consume, he hopes to inspire a movement of creators who use their platforms to enrich and elevate their audiences.

Akshay Maharaj

Connecting Creators with the World Beyond Language Barriers

https://aviewint.com/

Akshay is the co-founder of Aview International, which enables global content monetization for content creators and enterprises. Launched in 2017 while in high school, Akshay gained early traction by working with superstar creators like Logan Paul, Mark Rober and Yes Theory. Today, Aview has generated over 1B international views. Outside of Aview, Akshay co-founded and launched his second venture, Avybe, a platform that enables content creators to monetize their superfans. In 2021, Avybe closed its seed round, led by Tim Drapers, a VC fund in Silicon Valley. Today, Akshay is continuing to grow Aview and scaling its operations.

Most Creators Stay Local — And It's Costing Them

In today's saturated content landscape, most creators focus on building an audience within a single language or region. While this approach can yield strong engagement at home, it leaves significant value on the table globally.

As Akshay Maharaj, co-founder of Aview International, explains, "The problem that we're solving currently right now is the inability for content creators to globalize their content and monetize international audiences."

The issue isn't just linguistic—it's structural. Creators and brands often concentrate their content on a single dominant language or market, missing opportunities in Spanish-speaking, Hindi-speaking, or Arabic-speaking regions. Basic translations and auto-subtitles fall short of capturing cultural nuance, leading to reduced engagement and limited monetization.

Even when translation is addressed, most creators overlook distribution. "It's one thing to just translate a video," Akshay notes. "But it's a second thing to make sure that video actually resonates into the global audience that it's being featured in." Without culturally adapted content and dedicated channels, creators risk losing traction abroad.

Aview Localizes, Distributes, and Builds International Community

Aview approaches globalization as a two-part process: localization and cultural connection. Their platform combines AI with local human expertise to help creators become global storytellers—not just content exporters.

On the service side, Aview offers dubbing, transcription, and translation. But the real differentiator lies in how they manage and distribute localized content. Rather than pushing translated versions to a single channel, Aview creates new, audience-specific channels and adapts content to local preferences. "If I created a new Logan Paul international channel and culturally modified the lingo... he can then resonate with brands, with audience members, build a community," Akshay explains.

This model enables creators to launch and grow in new markets with content that feels native. AI helps speed up production, while local agencies and individuals ensure tone and messaging are culturally tuned. "We leverage local talents... to help us distribute that content," Akshay says.

Feedback from global viewers is a core part of the process. Aview monitors comment sections and user engagement to improve accuracy and connection. "We adjust the audio, reupload it... very simple," Akshay adds. This continuous improvement loop ensures the content remains relevant, authentic, and impactful.

A Borderless Future for Creators and Learners Alike

While Aview's immediate impact is expanding creator reach and revenue, its long-term vision is even more transformative. Akshay imagines a world where content flows freely across cultures and platforms—without language barriers.

"I want to just consume good content... without understanding as to the culture behind that," he says. In that vision, content becomes universally accessible, seamlessly adapted to the viewer's context. The implications go far beyond entertainment.

Aview is already investing in ed tech—bringing academic content across borders. "Imagine someone in the Middle East learning from a Harvard Business School professor," Akshay says. By removing language barriers, Aview is making global knowledge exchange possible.

"Right now, the biggest barrier for people working with other people is language," he reflects. "What if we remove that?"

By combining AI, cultural intelligence, and creator-first strategy, Aview is building the infrastructure for a borderless internet. For creators, this means unlocking new audiences. For the world, it means unlocking new potential.

Matt Panousis

MARZ Brings Dubbed Films Back to Life with AI

https://monstersaliensrobotszombies.com/

Matt is the co-founder and COO of Monsters Aliens Robots Zombies (MARZ). Prior to launching MARZ in 2018, he co-founded Toronto-based SaaS company ACTO. Matt holds a Juris Doctor degree from Queen's University and was named an EY Entrepreneur of the Year Ontario Finalist in 2023.

Dubbed Dialogue Breaks the Spell When It Doesn't Sync

As global streaming services expand, dubbed content reaches more audiences than ever. Yet, poorly synced dubs often shatter immersion, frustrating viewers with mismatched dialogue and facial movements. Matt Panousis, co-founder of MARZ, recalls, 'We all watched Squid Games and felt that visceral frustration when the lips don't match the dialogue.' Recognizing this issue as part of broader inefficiencies in the VFX industry—slow, labour-intensive, and costly processes—Matt and his team decided to change the game. By leveraging artificial intelligence, MARZ makes VFX faster and more affordable, ensures seamless dubs, and enhances the global storytelling experience.

AI-Powered Precision Makes Dubs Seamless and Stories Universal

"We developed a product that allows Hollywood studios to input new audio tracks for their dubs, and we recreate the facial movements," says Matt. Using advanced AI technology, LipDub AI precisely matches dubbed content to the original performance, ensuring the visuals align seamlessly in any language. By perfecting the synchronization of facial movements and dialogue, LipDub AI enhances the global appeal of content, creating immersive experiences that transcend language barriers.

Achieving this precision requires focusing on more than just the mouth. Matt explains, "We go from the eyes down to avoid sending the network contradictory signals." By ensuring that all expressions, from subtle eye movements to facial muscle shifts, are natural and consistent, MARZ avoids the "uncanny valley effect," where partially animated faces can appear artificial or unsettling. This level of detail ensures that viewers cannot distinguish between the original performance and the AI-driven dub, creating a truly immersive experience and setting a new standard for quality.

In the past, creating visual effects required months of work from large teams of VFX artists. With MARZ's AI-powered solutions, these effects can be completed in just a few keystrokes. The results must meet the industry's highest standards to gain acceptance in Hollywood. "We solve very specific applications, and we try to solve them end to end," says Matt, emphasizing the precision needed to meet these demands. AI tools like Vanity AI, which "save about 90 percent of the time that VFX artists traditionally spend," maintain Hollywood-quality output while drastically reducing production time.

A Future Where Anyone Can Create and Everyone Can Connect

MARZ's technology is also affordable, making high-quality VFX accessible to everyone. As Matt puts it, "A 13-year-old kid with a vision can now create something that visually matches a Hollywood film." This opens up opportunities for creators of all sizes. YouTubers who previously couldn't afford professional VFX can now use MARZ's tools to enhance their content, adding a level of polish that was once unattainable. By levelling the playing field, MARZ empowers creators across the industry to produce stunning, professional-grade work, fostering a new wave of creativity.

Matt Panousis believes that AI-driven VFX technology transforms content creation and connects global audiences like never before. "By removing the barriers of language and production costs, we're increasing accessibility and cultural relevance," he says. His belief that technology would continue to advance—and disrupt the industry—has driven MARZ's success. As MARZ pushes the limits of what AI can achieve, they are shaping a future where storytelling has no boundaries, bringing people closer through high-quality, shared media experiences.

6. EMPOWERING HEALTHCARE FOR EFFICIENCY AND ACCESSIBILITY

Leaders here are reimagining healthcare by empowering professionals with AI tools and innovative solutions that reduce inefficiencies and enhance patient care. Their work focuses on creating a healthcare system that's more accessible, resilient, and patient-centered.

Eunice Wu

Empowering Pharmacists with AI for a More Accessible Healthcare Future

https://www.asepha.ai

Eunice is the co-founder and CEO of Asepha, providing AI infrastructure to pharmacy software for streamlining clinical workflows. Asepha has gained early traction by working with publicly traded and Fortune50 pharmacy companies, and is on track to serve 30 million patients in 2025. Eunice holds a Doctor of Pharmacy degree from the University of British Columbia.

A Healthcare System Overwhelmed by Shortages and Inefficiencies

The healthcare system faces a daunting challenge: a global shortfall of 15 million healthcare workers by 2030, placing enormous pressure on existing professionals. Pharmacists, who have stepped up to fill critical gaps in primary care, are increasingly burdened by administrative tasks. "Pharmacists are moving more into a clinical role, but a lot of pharmacists are overwhelmed, overburdened," explains Eunice Wu, CEO of Asepha. With recent regulations allowing pharmacists to take on prescribing roles, their responsibilities are expanding, but they lack the support to make this shift sustainable. Wu notes, "I may be spending around 80 percent of my time on manual work, and only 20 percent of my time was being used on actual clinical services." The current reality means pharmacists are losing valuable time to mundane tasks, which could be automated to improve patient care and prevent burnout.

AI Solutions to Streamline Pharmacy Operations

Asepha is tackling these challenges with AI-driven clinical tools designed specifically for pharmacy workflows. "We create these AI clinical tools that help with manual tasks such as researching and documentation, and we allow these pharmacists to get closer to that 100 percent patient-facing care," says Wu. By automating non-clinical duties like documentation, medication reconciliation, and communication with other healthcare providers, Asepha's AI tools are revolutionizing the efficiency of pharmacies. These modular AI agents act like "Lego blocks," each handling distinct tasks, whether transcribing consultations or analyzing medication interactions. Processes like medication review, which took up to 45 minutes, can now be completed in 15 minutes using Asepha's technology. This significant reduction in time allows pharmacists to focus on what truly matters—providing personalized, direct patient care.

A Vision of Independent, Patient-Centric Pharmacies

Eunice Wu envisions a transformative future where pharmacists are empowered to act as independent healthcare providers, running self-sufficient pharmacies with minimal support staff. "I envision every pharmacist becoming their own pharmacy... automation helps perform the intake, helps triage the patients," Wu explains. This vision of AI-enhanced pharmacy transforms the pharmacist's role from an overburdened healthcare worker to a primary care provider capable of managing patients comprehensively. In this future, pharmacies become local healthcare hubs where patients can receive immediate care without long waits. "I genuinely see pharmacists becoming the new family physician," says Wu. By integrating advanced AI, Asepha aims to create a more accessible and efficient healthcare system where pharmacists fill the gaps left by physician shortages, ultimately elevating patient care and community health outcomes.

7. CYBERSECURITY AND DIGITAL RESILIENCE

This category encompasses leaders focused on fortifying digital infrastructure and protecting businesses against emerging cyber threats. Their innovations address the complexity of modern cybersecurity, balancing proactive defenses with system-wide resilience.

Ian
Amit

Closing the Gap Between Security and Innovation

gomboc.ai

Ian is the Co-Founder and CEO of Gomboc.ai who are providing cloud infrastructure security solutions.

Before Gomboc.ai, Ian served as a CSO/CISO for 5 years, held senior leadership positions with Rapid7, Cimpress, Amazon, ZeroFOX, IOActive and has over 25 years of experience in the security industry as a practitioner.

Ian is also the co-founder of DC9723 - the Tel Aviv DEFCON group-and serves as a BSides Las Vegas board member.

He is also the creator and co-CEO of The CISO Track - a series of CISO centric curated events, as well as an IANS faculty member.

Too Many Alerts, Too Few Solutions

Cloud security today is bogged down by inefficiencies. Security teams are overwhelmed by a never-ending backlog of alerts and lack the authority or knowledge to fix underlying architectural problems. This results in dependency on DevOps teams that are already stretched thin, causing crucial vulnerabilities to remain unresolved. As Ian Amit, CEO of Gomboc, puts it, "Security teams do not have the authority or the knowledge to actually make changes in cloud architecture, and they're dependent on DevOps. Without a clear path to a resolution, we're left scrambling." With cloud environments expanding rapidly and AI making attacks more sophisticated, the need for a solution has never been greater.

Real Fixes, Not Just More Alerts

Gomboc addresses an untapped area of cloud security by focusing on remediation—providing real, actionable fixes instead of merely generating alerts. "We focus on cloud remediation, which means that we're providing actual fixes to problems in cloud architecture security. And those fixes are contextual. They fit the specific customer architecture and environment without breaking it while delivering that gap closure," Ian explains. Gomboc uses deterministic AI to accurately resolve issues without risking disruption. Their AI-driven approach is designed to handle cloud misconfigurations and adapt to evolving cloud environments, eliminating the need for DevOps teams to deal with the intricacies of every security alert. Gomboc's methodology ensures that security measures are continually updated to align with the latest cloud services and configurations, allowing DevOps to focus on innovation and scaling rather than spending valuable time on repetitive security tasks.

A Future Where AI Empowers, Not Overwhelms

Ian Amit envisions a future where AI empowers defenders rather than attackers. AI has given malicious actors an edge, but Ian is optimistic about a shift in this balance. "The use of AI has really benefited the attackers more than the defenders," he says, but he sees an opportunity for AI to help defenders regain control. At Gomboc, the focus is on deterministic AI—a precise, engineered approach to cloud security. "Let me free you up from dealing with the nuances of the small things. These are the tasks that AI can really help us with," Ian says. His vision is to remove the low-hanging fruit of cloud vulnerabilities, allowing professionals to focus on higher-level challenges. In this future, cloud security will become proactive, operational teams will work more efficiently, and endless security concerns will no longer stifle innovation.

8. ROBOTICS AND AUTOMATION DRIVING THE NEXT INDUSTRIAL REVOLUTION

This category highlights leaders transforming industries through robotics and automation. By developing cutting-edge automation tools, they are enabling businesses to become more efficient, adaptive, and scalable, helping industries keep pace with the demands of the modern world.

Étienne Lacroix
Cutting Manufacturing Costs with Self-Serve Automation Tools

https://vention.io

"Business leader and entrepreneur building and turning around engineering-intensive businesses. I'm the founder and CEO of Vention, a Manufacturing Automation Platform that democratizes access to industrial automation. Today Vention serves 4,000 manufacturers over 25 industries and 30+ countries."

- Vention was named one of Canada's Top Growing Companies of 2023 by The Globe and Mail. Ranking #64 out of 425 companies

The High Costs and Complexity of Industrial Automation

Industrial automation is still out of reach for many small and medium-sized manufacturers today. The custom-built nature of manufacturing assets makes automation expensive and highly complex, often requiring a system integrator to design, program, and deploy each unique setup. "Most small and medium manufacturers just can't pay for it," explains Étienne Lacroix, founder and CEO of Vention. For these businesses, the high upfront cost of integrating automation technology means they are often left behind, struggling with labour shortages and unable to optimize their production processes. The existing automation landscape has, until now, favoured large corporations with deep pockets, leaving smaller manufacturers without the tools to compete effectively.

Making Automation Accessible with Self-Serve Technology

Vention is on a mission to democratize industrial automation. "We're making industrial automation accessible to all manufacturers," says Lacroix. With Vention's self-serve platform, manufacturing professionals can go online, design, program, and deploy automation systems alone without needing expensive third-party integrators. The platform serves a wide range of users, from shop-floor experts who understand their processes but lack formal engineering training to seasoned roboticists looking for a streamlined approach. "The key is making the user experience a zero-learning curve for those with manufacturing knowledge," Lacroix emphasizes. Vention's approach has helped countless small and medium-sized businesses get started with automation for the first time, significantly reducing costs and barriers to adoption.

As Lacroix envisions, the future also involves removing capital expenditure (CapEx) barriers entirely by moving towards virtualized machine design. "We need to finalize the step to virtualize machine design," he says. By using digital twins—virtual models of physical systems—manufacturers can test and debug their setups before any physical investment is made. "Test before you invest," Lacroix insists, pointing to the benefits of simulation and virtual troubleshooting as a game-changer that could make automation even more accessible and reduce financial risks for smaller companies.

A Future of Scalable, Autonomous Manufacturing

Étienne Lacroix's vision for the future of manufacturing goes beyond just reducing costs—it's about fundamentally changing how automation is approached. "The next big step is moving towards autonomous machines," he says. While full autonomy might still be a few years away, Lacroix sees incremental advances, such as machines capable of handling some functions autonomously, as the immediate next frontier. "Today, we're working on creating higher-level abstraction functions for robots, moving from prescriptive programming to mission-based tasks," he explains. This evolution will empower manufacturers to solve complex problems faster and with fewer resources.

When Vention reaches its goal of becoming IPO-ready, Lacroix envisions a world where manufacturers can quickly solve automation problems, seeing Vention's distinctive blue machines on factory floors worldwide. "Let's Vention this" is already becoming a term among clients, reflecting the ease and empowerment that Vention brings. Lacroix aims to make Vention synonymous with simple, effective, and scalable automation, enabling even the smallest manufacturers to compete globally and ushering in a new era of democratized, efficient, and resilient industrial production.

Wayne McIntyre

Reinventing Food Production Through Local Micro-Factories

https://www.relocalize.com/

Leader with a proven track record of accelerating sales growth, building high performing teams and developing revenue generating partnerships. Trusted advisor to CEOs and senior executives on growth strategy, growth leadership and sales acceleration. Proven transformational leader across multiple industries in various CXO-level roles.

Centralized Food Production Is Unsustainable

The global food production industry faces challenges threatening profitability and the planet's future. With inflation rising and supply chains strained, aspects of sustainability such as reducing carbon emissions, minimizing waste, and ensuring resource efficiency have shifted from distant goals to urgent necessities. 'Food retailers face inflation, supply chain control issues, disruptions, and a growing focus on sustainability,' says Wayne McIntyre, CEO of Relocalize. The stakes are enormous: centralized food production is responsible for 3.1 gigatons of annual CO_2 emissions. This is nearly three times that of the commercial aviation industry. This highlights the food industry's significant impact on global carbon levels, making it clear that a shift towards decentralized and sustainable production models is necessary before the environmental and financial costs become unbearable.

Wayne McIntyre and Relocalize are not just adapting—they are transforming food production. Recognizing the flaws in the centralized model, McIntyre and his team are creating 'micro-factories'—small-scale production units near distribution centers. These micro-factories eliminate long-haul transportation, significantly reducing the carbon footprint and creating a more sustainable and efficient food system.

"Centralization was built on the assumption of unlimited resources and cheap, available labour," McIntyre explains. However, this model no longer works in a world of finite resources and rising labour costs. Relocalize addresses these challenges by decentralizing production and creating a system that aligns with today's economic and environmental realities. This is not just an improvement—it's a complete transformation of food production and distribution.

Automation: The Power of Robotics in Decentralization

Relocalize's strategy centers on using advanced robotics to power autonomous micro-factories. McIntyre's vision is to revolutionize food production by bringing manufacturing closer to consumers and automating the process with modern technology. This approach streamlines production, reduces labour requirements, and ensures consistent, high-quality standards. By leveraging automation, Relocalize operates local production units as efficiently as large factories while significantly reducing costs and emissions. The result is a more flexible and sustainable food system.

Targeting the Right Products: Packaged Foods and Water-Heavy Goods

"We focus on packaged foods because they offer high throughput," McIntyre says. Shipping water-heavy products like beverages and ice over long distances is both costly and environmentally inefficient. Relocalize's micro-factories near distribution hubs address this issue by producing these goods locally, reducing transportation inefficiencies. Furthermore, the decentralized model provides resilience during disasters. "If a hurricane affects part of the network, other parts can compensate," McIntyre notes, ensuring continuity even in crises.

A Mission to Decarbonize the Food System

"Our primary purpose as an organization is decarbonization," says McIntyre. This mission drives their vision of establishing a network of micro-factories across North America, each designed for maximum carbon and cost efficiency. By producing food locally, Relocalize reduces transportation emissions and builds a sustainable, resilient food system. McIntyre envisions a future where food is produced close to where it is consumed, cutting emissions and operational costs while meeting the growing demand for sustainability.

Relocalize isn't just responding to change but leading it—creating a food system fit for the 21st century.

AFTERTHOUGHT

Your Future Narrator Journey Starts Now

Throughout this book, we've explored how bold declarations, thought leadership, and innovation can change industries, impact lives, and leave a lasting legacy.

The journey of a Future Narrator requires courage, a willingness to challenge the status quo, and the strategic mindset to share your vision across multiple platforms. This book has provided you with the frameworks and practical steps to start your journey—from crafting your strategic narrative and leveraging the power of podcasting to creating enduring legacy content that positions you as a category-defining leader.

But the journey does not end here.

Becoming a Future Narrator is about consistent, intentional action—taking your vision from inspiration to real-world impact. As a CEO or founder, you have a unique opportunity to stop competing in an industry and start defining it. The path to category creation is not easy, but it is one of immense reward and influence. It is for those ready to embrace leadership that sparks movements.

At this point, you have a choice:

- You can set this book down and continue with business as usual.

- Or you can take the next step to become the Future Narrator of your industry.

We've equipped you with the tools, insights, and real-world examples of leaders who have successfully built and mobilized their own categories. Now it's your turn.

What's Next?

- **One Place for Everything**

  Your journey as a Future Narrator doesn't stop here.

  Get all the worksheets, access exclusive insights, and learn how to work with us—all in one place.

The future isn't something to react to—it's something you create.
Go forward and design the world you're innovating for.

Implementing & Scaling Your Future Narrative
Scan the QR Code below or visit

Bookmark this page so you can return anytime and continue building your Future Narrative.

resources.futurenarrator.com/hub

ABOUT THE AUTHORS

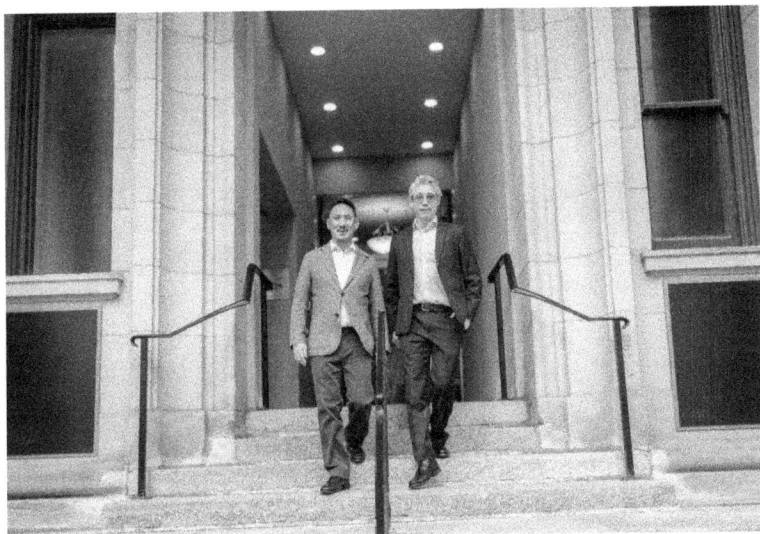

EDWIN J. FRONDOZO (LEFT)

Edwin J. Frondozo is a visionary tech entrepreneur, award-winning podcaster, and co-founder of Slingshot, a B2B voice communications platform. As the founder of The Business Leadership Podcast, he has interviewed over 300 pioneering leaders from companies like Google, Microsoft, and Wealthsimple—providing insights on leadership, innovation, and transformation. His podcast has earned multiple accolades, including Podcast of the Year and ranking among the Top 10 Best Business Podcasts.

As the co-creator of the Future Narrator Framework, Edwin helps leaders craft their Future Point of View (POV) to produce podcasts that spark conversations, shape industries, and drive innovation. He has collaborated with global brands like RBC, Mastercard, and Intel to develop impactful thought leadership initiatives. Active within Canada's startup ecosystem, Edwin mentors emerging entrepreneurs and fosters dialogue on the evolving landscape of leadership and business.

DR. PAUL NEWTON (RIGHT)

Dr. Paul Newton is a master storyteller, book strategist, and publishing expert specializing in branding, thought leadership, and category creation. With a background in healthcare and a passion for understanding human motivation, he transitioned from a career in chiropractic to coaching and consulting, helping leaders articulate their unique value and build meaningful narratives. Through his work with founders, CEOs, and industry pioneers, he has developed systems to craft compelling stories that drive engagement, position brands, and create lasting impact. His work has helped company founders secure millions of dollars in investment, attract the best and brightest talent, and deliver the talk of a lifetime on the TEDx stage. He is the co-creator of the Future Narrator Framework, guiding leaders in building category-defining movements.

ACKNOWLEDGMENTS

We are deeply grateful for the incredible support, feedback, and inspiration that made this book possible. Each contribution—whether through direct insight, shared experience, or the strength of community—has helped shape this project into what it is today.

Direct Contributors & Feedback Providers

Amanda Annis – For supporting us from day one, organizing our presence at the Collision Conference event, and ensuring that things went flawlessly.

Anand Murthy - provided feedback

Draga Jovanovic - For taking amazing photographs and turning us into models.

Hamza Khan – For taking the time to read and provide comprehensive thoughts and suggestions on improving.

Joel Macharles – Provided invaluable manuscript feedback and creative insights.

Kevin Dubrosky – For providing keen insights and making sure the book sounds like "Edwin."

Luis Muñoz – For taking our frameworks and applying them right away, providing us early acceptance.

Paddy Cosgrave – For founding Collision Conference and Web Summit, providing an incredible platform for founders, CEOs, and innovators to connect and share their stories.

Ron McCormack – For helping refine key ideas on improving the book.

Samantha Lloyd - For collaborating and providing key feedback and insights.

Shafin Jadavji - For sharing his beautiful space to take amazing photos.

Stella Mariz Nadela – For putting it all together.

Tara McEwan – For taking time to read and review the book.

Tenzin Lobsang – For designing the book cover and advising on how to layout the book.

Support & Community Groups

Entrepreneurs & Notable Friends:

Bonnie Chan

Carol Moxam

Catherine Tanaka

Darryl Bandoro

David Setiadi

Dave Ross

Derek Viverios

Eric Rafat

Flavio Rosetto

Haseeb Awan

Jody Laraya

Josh Almario

Josh Leslie

Kaye Peñaflor

Keka DasGupta

Kira Day

Koppel Halshtok

Linda North

Mike Damphousse

Shyra Barberstock

Stephen DeWitt

Suzanne Grant

Tahani Aburaneh

Theresa Laurico

Tuan Nguyen

Walid Al-Hajj

Entrepreneurial Networks:

These are organizations, mastermind groups, and professional communities that have supported the journey.

Brampton Entrepreneur Centre

DDG Mastermind

Empact Ventures

FoundersBeta

Futurepreneur

Global Startups (formerly Latam Startups)

Inner Tribe Community

Mastermind Dinners

My Advisory Board Group of Hooligans and Yahoos (aka The Tuanitos)

Passion Centre

Speaker Slam

Startup Canada

Techstars

The Podcast Academy

Twitch Business Mastermind

The Business Leadership Podcast community

Livecasts.fm network
Podcasters Mastermind
Socialite Community

Local & Community Networks:

Kalayaan Cultural Community Centre
Running Room run clubs
Toronto Go-Getters Toastmasters

INDEX

T

V

W

NOTES:

For information about the authors, see About the Authors.

See Also Cross-References:

- Future Vision — see also: Narrative Design, Strategic Storytelling

- Point of View (POV) — see also: Founder POV, Thought Leadership

- Evangelization — see also: Movement Building, Community Engagement

- Storytelling — see also: Narrative Arc, Authenticity in Thought Leadership

- Frameworks (General) — see also: Future Narrative Framework, Evangelization Pillars

Final Thanks

*Thank you to everyone—each individual and group—
for your trust, encouragement, and shared passion.
Your contributions, both big and small, have been
essential to bringing this book to life.*

www.ingramcontent.com/pod-product-compliance
Lightning Source LLC
Chambersburg PA
CBHW030331220326
41518CB00048B/2228